Salt
and
Roses

The Coastal Maine Way of Life

Other books by Islandport Press

Whatever It Takes
May Davidson

My Life in the Maine Woods
Annette Jackson

Nine Mile Bridge
Helen Hamlin

In Maine
John N. Cole

Stories of Aroostook
Kathryn Olmstead

Evergreens
John Holyoke

Old Maine Woman
Glenna Johnson Smith

These and other books are available at:
www.islandportpress.com

Salt *and* *Roses*

The Coastal Maine Way of Life

MAY DAVIDSON

ISLANDPORT PRESS

ISLANDPORT PRESS

PO Box 10
Yarmouth, Maine 04096
www.islandportpress.com
info@islandportpress.com

ISBN: 978-1-952143-17-5
ebook ISBN: 978-1-952143-30-4
Library of Congress Control Number: 2021932275
Printed in the USA

Dean Lunt, Publisher
Teresa Lagrange, Book design
Cover art by Suzi Thayer

Dedication

To my beloved Connie and Paul, who bring me laughter, inspiration, purpose, joy, courage, and who enfold me in their deep and tender love each day. They are my life's blessings, the sun and stars that light my pathways

TABLE OF CONTENTS

PROLOGUE

Salt and Roses is a collection of true stories, mostly comical, about situations my husband Jim and I, along with many others, have experienced. These are the salt part of this book. The roses are based on my observations of nature's beauty and mystery.

There is a second reason for *Salt and Roses* as a title. We spent some of our happiest days exploring Maine's many islands. During the summer, their harbors and coves are drenched in the memory-inspiring scent of salt air and the wild rugosa roses that grow thick on island shores. These fragrances became the base for an enduring recollection of near-perfect times in our lives.

I had to wait until I was sixteen to have my mother explain why I was so infatuated with a particular island in Muscongus Bay. My mother was born in Scotland in 1904. Her upbringing leaned toward old Victorian attitudes about personal subjects. When I was a child, my parents and I lived in the coastal town of Bremen, and our house sat at the edge of Greenland Cove. Whenever we rowed the dory out to this island in the bay for a picnic, I didn't want to leave it. I still don't.

For my sixteenth birthday, we planned a visit to *my* island and at that point Mother felt it was time to tell me exactly why I am so attached to it. She said, in the summer of 1928, she and my father were out exploring the island and became, in her words, "very friendly." The result of that friendly encounter was my appearance

May and Jim Davidson

nine months later in May 1929. I must have been waiting on the shore among the spruce trees and wild roses.

My parents, John and Jo Banis, owned a saltwater farm and small summer guest inn named Mayfair House. My childhood was idyllic. I learned to work, appreciate and love the natural world that surrounded us of sea and forest, and soak up a unique kind of education from the fine guests at the inn. Best of all, one summer I met Jim, my life's love and mate.

I was just sixteen when Jim and his Aunt Clara came to stay for a week at our Inn. When my mother introduced us, it was love at first sight. Jim was my first and only love. On the last day of his stay,

Jim and I spent a glorious day on Hog Island. We walked every trail, examined the wonders washed up on the shores, climbed the ledges and rocks, waded on the beaches, and built elaborate sandcastles. We ate our lunch leaning against spruce trees, smelling the sea, and watching its diamonds glinting in a June sun. We enjoyed every moment with the only shadow the knowledge that Jim would likely be drafted later that summer.

When we were back on the mainland, there was still a beautiful walk along the field road and through the woods. With no spoken word, Jim took my hand, the first time we had touched, and continuing to hold hands as we sauntered toward home discussing the beauties of a day spent in an island paradise. The following day Jim and his Aunt Clara had to leave on an early train. In a private moment, Jim held me and kissed me tenderly, promising me that somehow, in some way he would return, and he hoped that I would wait for him. Silently I nodded my agreement, and then he was gone.

He kept his promise, returning for a visit that summer and then for good after his discharge. From that beginning, we enjoyed a wonderfully adventurous life together for sixty-eight years.

This book of true stories covers decades of memories, of summers at the inn, around the farm on boats, and some of the many adventures we enjoyed in and out of Maine. Since I am now in my tenth decade, it's time to share some of the fun.

About that tenth decade—I also want to share some thoughts on that. Please, embrace your advancing years. Have no fear. We all go through our destinies of angst, grief, and joy, but then love and laughter will also carry us onward. Remember—after every sunset comes another sunrise.

Even better if its on a magical island filled with the sweet air of salt and roses.

OCTOBER, SUMMER'S SUNSET

All through my many decades, I have marveled at how quickly summer passes. October comforts us for this loss, enchanting us with new beauty, a yearly display of rampant and glorious color. As we clean out the gardens and mow the lawn perhaps one last time, we must stop, breathe in the wonder of the trees so soothingly green all summer, now shades of topaz, merlot, rubies, and Egyptian gold. Their hues are even more vivid against pines and balsam. Milkweed pods and goldenrod grace the fields and lakes that are now October's shade of deep indigo.

I can't pass a window without being drawn to the daily changes of the leaves. Too soon they begin to drift toward earth in a lazy zigzag or fly in abundance, torn loose by a sudden breeze, sweeping across fields, or coming to rest against a stonewall. They will nourish the earth wherever they fall.

The gray of leafless hardwoods is brightened and softened by the perpetual green of our great pines and spruce. In the twilight hour after sunset the autumn sky will be its seasonal shades of dusky rose and amethyst.

The earth of the North still provides for us even when winter's frozen depth arrives. Juniper bushes bear an abundance of blue-green berries, firm and smooth. Picking them from their prickly host is done slowly, allowing time to enjoy the hush of fall twilight while anticipating the spicy delight of juniper chicken jubilee.

Crush a few tablespoons of the berries with several garlic cloves, add them to undiluted frozen orange juice, a splash of lemon juice, and a dash of red pepper, pour over pieces of skinless chicken and bake in oven until done. Although the flavor is jubilant, perhaps the best part is harvesting the juniper berries in the magic of an autumn landscape.

The forest calls to be entered. Walk over silent pine needles and the papery crackle of dry leaves. Smile at the narrow trails of small animals, find moose tracks in damp ground, look overhead to see where his antlers may have snapped a few brittle branches as he traveled. Immerse yourself in the fragrance of the woods, a blend of nuts, evergreen resin, and moist earth. Leave this haven of nature with a sense of rapture in knowing it exists and that you may return in a few months to share in the forest's bounty of spring.

Soon the flaming torches of autumn color will turn to the fine ash gray of the hardwoods. A few slumbering coals of gold and russet leaves will cling to the oaks. October is summer's sunset, its last gift of glory for the season. Then it will be November, the month of twilight before the soft early darkness of winter's night and December's swirling snow.

Visit from the Forest King

There are times in your life when you are in desperate need of something to uplift your spirits and it actually appears. We had such an experience one memorable October evening at our farm in Round Pound. Our apple trees, only twenty feet from our house, were more loaded with fruit than we had ever seen them. Big, bright red McIntosh apples hung from every branch.

Late on a dimly moonlit night, Jim glanced outside and saw long white legs slowly moving under the apple trees. He watched as they progressed and saw that they were attached to a huge, dark body. He woke me so we could discover what this creature might be together. When it stepped into the light from our house, we saw that it was a magnificent bull moose. His rear legs were white from just above the hocks to his hooves, and his front legs were white up to the back of his knees.

He reached into the branches of the tree to snap off an apple, then lowered his great antlered head to chew his prize. He took about four crunches, light steam clouds escaping from his mouth with each swing of his jaws. He was so close we could see how his square upper lip hung over the lower one, giving him the moose's signature hooked nose.

The moose's motion was slow and methodical. We watched him with awe and delight as he completed the round of the three trees, plucking apples from his stately height.

When he began to leave the trees, we were sure he would go back to the woods. He went only a few steps before folding his long legs to make a smooth descent to the grassy lawn near our big windows.

He lay facing the woods with his back to us and began chewing his cud. His long ears and beautiful palmed rack wiggled as he chewed. Sometimes he turned his head in profile so we could see his wondrous triangular beard also swaying. We continued observing him from the darkened room, solemnly inspired by the majesty of his presence, by his gift of primal beauty, by his fearlessness to lay so close to us. There was an urge to take a picture of the moose so we could believe he had actually been there, but we could not bear to violate his presence with a bright flash. This appearance was too precious.

We went back to bed feeling like our hours observing the splendor of this great being and his apparent trust were an omen of joy for us. He had come to show us a beauty seldom seen and experienced in the way that we just had, delivering a special message for us.

That sense stayed with us all the next day. We went outside to see the area where the moose's big body had melted the frost under it. We yearned for him to come again, but did not expect it. Still, we watched until late the next night and were exultant to see him under the apple trees again, gently pulling the fruit he so enjoyed.

Once more, he lay down facing the woods in nearly the same spot on the lawn and began chewing his cud. Several hours later we left the bed again to see him still there. By this time his massive head was drooping with sleep, and we wondered how he held up the great weight of his antlers when in repose. A few moments later he swung his head toward his shoulder and, although it was hard to be certain, he seemed to rest his head while propping the tip of an antler on the ground.

The moose brought us this bounty of joy each night for several more nights performing in the same way—munching apples, then lying down to enjoy his cud, and taking a long nap. When he had eaten all the hanging fruit he could reach in the tree, he began nuzzling up those that had fallen to the ground. The valuable lesson seemed to be even when you have consumed the best, enjoy the rest. He also never ate more than he needed during a visit. We looked forward to staying up a few hours each night to watch this splendid being, to absorb and wonder at the magic of his presence. Every morning at daylight the moose would rise and follow his same path through the nearby pines, halfway around the farm pond, and then disappear into the thick growth of fir trees.

One night about a week later, he didn't visit the apple trees and we mourned, although we always knew that time would come. Then, while seated at our large window having breakfast, the moose ambled along his trail in the bright of day and ate a few apples from the ground. Several of his poses proved good for pictures, and we happily used the camera through the windows. When he was finished eating, he looked gently at us with a full forward gaze, then slowly turned and walked a different path to the back of the pond. He took a long time to travel the back pasture and head northward into the big woods.

The moose seemed to convey to us he was moving on. Even though there were still plenty of apples, he had spent enough time here with us and now must go. He had accomplished his mission to bring us a gift of beauty and faith. Our thoughts were filled with emotion and thankfulness for this mystical experience provided by the majesty and dignity of this great king of the forest. It was akin to a religious presentation and will be with us always.

As he glided into the big pines we whispered an entreaty for his enduring safety, and we thought of the words that, in lore, are believed the moose imparts: "Help me to honor the gifts I can give and recognize my worthiness as long as I live."

Maine Wilderness Adventure

When I think of a wilderness, I get lost in the glory of the word. I am deeply comforted to know that Maine has ten million acres of it. May it always be so.

During an early November in the fifties. A small group of good friends, eight of us in total, decided that our winter food supply should be enhanced since deer hunting season had just begun. Why not combine a fun camping trip into the wild with the practical goal of finding food for our families!

.None of us had camping equipment. We had neither the time or money for that pastime, but no matter. Bob, our leader, believed the Allagash region was the place to go, as it was probably stiff with deer and a shelter of sorts could be arranged. He located a camp some fifty miles off into the Allagash wilderness. It was part of what was left from an old logging operation.

Half the fun of such an expedition is the preparation—planning food to bring, pots, pans, bedding, and clothing. Nobody had sleeping bags, so there were many blankets and pillows. One couple couldn't sleep without taking their own mattress. It became necessary to hitch a two-wheel trailer behind Bob's big station wagon.

The car and trailer were stacked high and tied down with enough rope to anchor a cargo ship. There is no question that we looked like the Beverly Hillbillies going up the road. But we were a happy bunch, laughing, teasing, and filled with the spirit of adventure in the wilderness.

We left well before dawn and headed to Patten, near the way into the Allagash region. It was almost sunset when we arrived at the camp after negotiating about fifty miles of the narrow ninety-mile logging road into the wilderness. The camp was better described as a shack, but it had bunks, a small wood stove, and an outhouse of sorts.

After unloading our household on wheels and eating sandwiches while working, we selected our bunks and fell into them. Sleep came quickly after the long trip, in the deep silence of the woods.

At sunrise, the men went out to gather more firewood while the women made breakfast. We asked each fellow how he wanted his eggs. There were orders for fried, scrambled, boiled, over easy, etc. When they returned with the wood, every egg was fried to blackened edges. Orders were ignored. The tiny wood stove didn't make variety possible beyond the capacity of two big frying pans.

Soon we all set out down the logging road to look for deer signs. I have never gone hunting to shoot anything, always just to go along and enjoy the woods. We spent the day exploring, only leaving the road for short distances, and using compasses to orient ourselves. We understood that from where we were, one could walk a straight line in the forest for three weeks before arriving in Canada.

This wilderness was a breathtaking place. Evergreens were so tall that their tops formed a canopy, and even in the sunny daylight it felt like we were walking in twilight. The fragrance of fir and pine was a living presence. We were drenched in lonely and primal beauty, profound silence, and awed by our insignificance in this vast forest.

The only animal sign the first day was a pile of steaming moose droppings near some white cedar trees. The next day there wasn't even that. There was no evidence of deer or that they had ever been there. The country is so huge their range can be endless.

At nights we ate potluck in the camp or whatever the two fry pans would produce, played rousing card games, and went to bed early, pleasantly tired from a full day of tramping the forest and enjoying its magnificence.

The third morning we awoke to six inches of snow on the ground and more coming down hard and fast. Well! We hadn't thought of this. Not one of us. Down state it wasn't snow time yet. No snow shovels, no snow tires or chains for the station wagon. Nothing to do but leave as fast as we could pile our copious stuff into the trailer and wagon. This was accomplished with the speed of a fast-forwarded movie.

Then we faced what passed for a road. The first few miles were fairly level, but after that it was hill after hill. With summer-smooth tires and a heavy trailer, Bob's station wagon wanted to remain in place with wheels spinning in the snow.

The scene for the next fifty miles went like this: All the men except Bob, who was the driver, put their shoulders and arms to the rear of the wagon and trailer, pushing mightily. The women dug into the trailer for pans, pots, spatulas, large spoons, anything that would hold gravel or dirt. We trotted alongside the wagon throwing these meager contents in front of the rear wheels, then ran ahead to find more loose road material to fill our sanding equipment. The results were like trying to empty the ocean with a tea cup.

An image that remains with me is Bob's tiny wife dressed in a bright red hooded parka. She looked like a small elf as she dug vigorously for gravel with an egg lifter which was designed with many holes in its flat part. It held about a thimbleful, but she forged ahead, digging and running to the nearest tire.

Bob fought the station wagon along as men and women stumbled and strove through their assigned duties. Progress was less than slow. Then, in our exhausted state, we were treated to the final indignity caused by our lack of preparation.

A sporty powerful Jeep roared up behind us seeking to pass. State-of-the-art hunting and camping equipment was neatly stacked and secured to its roof. Its big tires were covered in shiny snow chains, and all wheels were sailing through the snow as if it didn't exist. The Jeep's license plate read California.

As it slowed to pass us, we had to step back beyond the narrow road's edge. Our men looked wistfully at the Jeep, and the women stood holding our road-building pots, pans, spoons, and spatulas. Taking all this in, the driver saw the Maine plate on the wagon and, shaking with laughter, he shouted, "I thought you people in Maine knew how to live here in snow!"

We watched as he sped off, showering us with more snow, and knew he would be regaling friends with his impression of Maine people in the Maine woods.

Tired but still laughing together, we arrived home just before dawn. No snow on the ground. As they approached their doorway one of our couples saw three deer under the apple trees just fifty yards from their house.

But why hunt close to home when you can tackle the Maine wilderness and show a Californian how a few of us Maine folks handle snow?

Shadows

Looking at the winter scene various times from dawn to sunset, I think about how it changes with directions of light. Woods, fields, and lawns are all in place, but shadows and reflections are like an artist's paints. Details are emphasized, objects are enhanced, and a certain magic is at work.

In moonlight, the stream in back of the house that flows between pines, birches, and firs is like a woodcut in blacks, grays, and smoke blues. By day, slanting rays of sun on its snowy surface cast lacy shadows of evergreen branches and dark tunnels among the tree trunks.

Early morning shadows are cheerful. The day is beginning with sunshine. I find that afternoon shadows are different. When they slant across a long, green lawn in summer while the day is ending, a feeling of nostalgia comes to me, a kind of tender anguish. It is a beautiful time of day, no reason for even that slight melancholy mixed with memory. Why? Perhaps because day's end is a measure of time, and now I wish to hoard time. More, I think it is because I know this exquisite moment of beauty cannot be held.

Memories surface with sun shadow scenes. One from the late 1930s I sometimes recall is a day with my parents, John and Jo Banis. It was a January thaw, the kind of day that inspired thoughts of distant spring. We lived at Greenland Cove, a reasonable rowing distance from Hog Island and the Audubon Nature Camp. Captain Davis, the camp's winter caretaker on the island, had invited us to visit. I was a little girl, and then, even as now, anything that involved a boat, saltwater, and an island was my idea of nirvana.

The dory ride over the silken waters from Greenland Cove to Hog Island was short, the turning tide rich in marine smell. This island, so close to land, is still a world in itself, a haven of thick forest and wildlife. Thawing snow brought forth the essence of cold earth and evergreen resin, the air sharp but salt-sweet with every breath. Winter silence prevailed on this calm day. Golden sun rays slanted through the dark, wet woods and beckoned exploration along their bright paths.

The visit with Captain Davis and his lovely wife passed too quickly. An amazing and memorable highlight was when the captain took a head of lettuce from their ice box, opened a kitchen window, and called out the names Peggy, Dot, and Sally several times. Soon three beautiful does appeared at the window to nibble happily at the chunks of lettuce he held for them. Their great soft eyes shone and white tails waved excitedly as they crunched on their welcome treat. The Davis family dwelled in a Maine Eden.

Now Winter

The first snowstorm is always exciting. It brings the challenge of battening down the hatches, watching the sky darken, and feeling that special stillness that prevails before the snow begins. The fine, powdery flakes usually predict a long storm with serious amounts of snow.

I love to hear the wind's early warning whispers in the spruces and pines. The frozen pond is the first to show the snow's arrival, as it sweeps and swirls across the sleek surface. The cold air is clean, fresh, and exhilarating before the comfort of coming inside a warm house to watch the power and force of a gathering blizzard.

Snow makes Christmastime seem real. How lucky we are to be able to step into our woods, find the perfect Christmas balsam, pine cones, and red winterberries, and be surrounded by the wondrous scents and scenes of an all natural Christmas. Lights and lawn ornaments are pretty and joyful, but for those of us who live in Maine, the real Christmas decor is all around us.

Some years we have been in New York City near Christmas time, attending trade shows for our North Country Wind Bell business. The scenes there are very different—neon glitz and glamour, elegantly dressed store windows with stunningly expensive offerings on display, roaring traffic, hordes of people rushing along sidewalks covered in filthy snow slush.

New York City has many levels of lifestyle, from the highest to the lowest. Most people are living regular lives and commute daily to their jobs in the smelly, cement canyons of the subway.

One vignette stays in my mind. Jim and I were hurrying through a cafeteria breakfast before going to the Jacob Javits Center, an event center in Manhattan, for a day's work at the trade show. A little old lady, raggedly dressed and not very clean, deposited a soiled canvas bag on a chair at her table. After bringing her tray of meager food, she opened the bag and took out ten small stuffed animals. They had all become the same color and were losing parts because of being handled often.

The lady placed them carefully in a semicircle around her plate and, eating slowly, she spoke to each one of them by name, giving pretend answers and carrying on a conversation. They were her family, obviously always with her. In this city of millions, this woman lived within walls of loneliness greater than if she were by herself in a beautiful tundra. We found it profoundly sad.

Everyone must live where they find happiness and fulfillment. I do realize that, but the following poem I found in an old *Farm Journal* over fifty years ago sums it up for me.

The Country Woman

My city sister pities me:
I who am comraded by rain
And sun and wind and all this free
Untrammeled space. She makes it plain
That city life holds many more "Fine, cultural advantages:
So many things that one can store
Within the heart,"—or so she says. She ends her visit and returns
To the din in which her life is spent,
And I who love the things she spurns,
Turn back to them still more content.

Moonlight and Icicles

During this open winter, the interaction of rising and lowering temperatures brings beauty to offset the changing surfaces of mud and snow. There is compensation for nearly every condition in nature. When it occurs, one of my delights is snow slowly melting from a metal roof. It slides a short distance in the sun, but the cooling evening causes it to hang outside the windows in a frozen valance.

A fringe of long icicles forms on this drapery and slowly drips. On moonlit nights they become enchanting. The movement of gradual melting creates internal bursts of color in the icicles. Fragmented rainbows dart from the slow drops. Shapes and brilliance shift by the moment. I am caught in a winter thrall of magic as I watch this display vary with each pale cloud that drifts across the moon.

On a cold sun and wind-sharp day I study the resident crows. They huddle tightly in the snow-covered field, dipping their beaks deep into a drift, then holding their heads straight up as they take in this needed moisture. Their ebony wings flash shades of wine in the sun. They are a small family enduring the elements in the togetherness of survival.

There is a wealth of peace and beauty on a winter night. The burning-blue radiance of moonlight on snow, tall, dark pines lifting the curves of their layered branches reaching for the sky in an attitude of worship.

Cold and night-deep silence prevails over field and forest except for the occasional lonely scream of a bobcat or the hushing sweep of owl wings as one glides to its favorite hunting perch in a mighty oak. From this vantage point he will watch for mice making snow tunnels. Even our harshest season provides the diamond edges of beauty.

1950's Wild Trip to the North Country

Bitter cold January days remind me of a trip Jim and I made many years ago to St. Marie de Kent in New Brunswick, Canada. It wasn't the time of year one would choose to go into that area, but it was necessary if we were to make the purchase of an outstanding stud ram that became available for sale.

We had brought the first flock of North Country Cheviot sheep into the eastern United States. This is a very old breed that originated in Scotland. We needed a new ram, and at that time North Country Cheviots were only in Canada. We had been in touch with the Canadian Department of Agriculture for help in our search for a ram with the particular breed character of the one now for sale.

He had been Grand Champion of his breed at the Royal Winter Fair in Toronto and was now to be sold by his owner at this remote New Brunswick farm. There was much interest in him, so it was a matter of not wasting time to go and see about him. He sounded like what we had been looking for to continue the traits we had begun in our ewe flock. The last week in January, we hastily prepared for the trip. We removed the backseat from the Chevrolet sedan and filled the empty space with straw, a few flakes of hay, and a water bucket.

Starting out before daylight, we kept a steady pace north until we met the Canadian Agriculture representative who was to guide us to the LeBlanc farm. He was to be our interpreter as well, for we do not speak French and the LeBlanc family didn't speak English.

After we expressed our feelings of inadequacy by needing an interpreter, our guide, Leo, assured us that proficiency in Parisian French would have been no help because even he had difficulties with the many changes in dialect within a one hundred mile area.

Because of the distance, it had been arranged that we would stay overnight with the LeBlanc family. We were given no directions to the farm. We were to follow Leo, who would also stay overnight. There were times when we yearned for directions, for keeping him in sight was like participating in the Grand Prix. The temperature on this early afternoon was twenty degrees below zero.

Accumulated winter snow still covered the land, making the naturally narrow roads mere slots. Leo believed in speed at any cost and we snaked up and down the hills, careened around curves, and thundered across one-way wooden bridges as if we were on the rails of a roller coaster. There were many junctions and side roads, and we knew if we lost Leo it would take days to find our way out of these unmarked roads. If there were signs, they were now buried beneath the snow.

Fear of following Leo was outweighed by fear of losing him, so we continued the insane pace for several hours until he came to a halt at the top of one of the endless hills. Nothing could be seen beyond the snow canyon the road had become. Leo announced that we had arrived and because of the depth of snow, we would have to leave the cars where they were and climb the steps carved into the snow bank to get to the farm.

What came into view was an isolated set of buildings—a house two small rooms wide and three stories high, a large barn, and several outbuildings high on the hill overlooking fields, dark forest, and a frozen river. The LeBlanc couple was smiling and gracious. Mr. LeBlanc was round-faced and sturdy, with large hands that delivered an iron grip of welcome. Mrs. LeBlanc was tall and sweetly shy with gray hair pulled into a severe bun.

After all those miles we were burning to see the ram, but custom required a meal first. It was suppertime by then and thirty degrees below zero. The pleasant wood cook stove warmed the tiny kitchen and our supper. The LeBlancs served varieties of home-canned vegetables, farm-smoked sausage, and baby clams with drawn butter alongside freshly baked bread. During the meal, Leo carried conversation in two languages while skillfully catching the LeBlancs up on provincial news.

When supper was cleared away, we adjourned to the one other first floor room: the parlor. It has always stayed in my memory. It had a small wood stove crouched in a corner with family pictures on the oatmeal-color papered walls. The only furniture consisted of twenty straight-backed wooden chairs squeezed together against the four walls. Dessert was solemnly served in the form of a large box of toothpicks passed around by Mrs. Leblanc. Never having need of these, we nearly declined, but instead we fortunately followed Leo's example and accepted one each.

A good half-hour followed while the bilingual conversation rose and fell. We sat rigidly upright in the hard chairs and smiled often to make up for our lack of speech. I watched in fascination as the LeBlancs laboriously probed the extremities of each tooth, letting not a morsel be lost. Looking about the stark room, I pictured its limited use in toothpick socials and wakes. There wasn't space for dancing after a wedding. However, this room held a depth of charm for the special meaning it held for the LeBlancs.

The unique entertainment was over when the toothpicks had become frayed stubs. Jim and I learned by observing how to roll the toothpicks around in our mouths as if we were enjoying them. At last, it was time to see the ram. The still outdoor air was so cold that breathing was painful, but inside the dimly lit barn the steaming, pleasant pungency of dairy cows and draft horses mixed with familiar sheep smells was warm and comforting.

Pointing to a pen constructed of wood rails, Leo said, "There is the ram." I thought there must be two animals in the pen standing end to end, but as we approached it was evident that it was only one large ram of great length. He was everything we had hoped for in size, quality, and breed character. It took only a few moments for us to know he was worth the trip.

We could have spent the remainder of the evening admiring the ram, but it was time to return to the kitchen and begin arriving at a price for him. Leo accomplished the awkward bargaining after a couple of hours. It was not until we left him in Moncton later that he told us Joe LeBlanc spoke no English but understood it very well. The transaction could have been shortened greatly had we known this, but it was all part of the ceremony—like the toothpicks.

Excited about our new ram, we sunk into the feather bed in a narrow upstairs room. The blankets were huge and heavy, and a tiny wood stove crackled beside us. Wood was piled alongside it. The stove was close to the wallpapered wall and there was no metal or brick protection under it, just the wood floor. Jim fed the stove through the night and we slept with one eye open in case of sparks.

The next day, we exchanged hearty hugs of adieu and merci and the ram struggled down the snow steps into the car. The thermometer read forty degrees below zero. Our Chevy responded with a single weary grunt and fell silent. Because of its automatic transmission, rolling it down the steep hill did nothing but get us to the bottom. No nice clutch and gear grab of a stick shift.

The nearest garage was miles away and Leo's car was too small to tow us. A neighbor with a pickup truck pulled us over hill and dale for miles before finally getting up enough momentum for the car's engine to catch. This trip inspired us to own nothing but pickup trucks with standard shifts for use as family cars.

Because of our delay in leaving Canada, the border veterinary inspection at St. Stephen was not possible as planned, and we had to drive many extra hours for entry through the larger port of Houlton, Maine. The extra fuel, payment to the neighbor who towed us, and overtime inspection fee sent us home supperless, but all that mattered was having this beautiful animal to join our flock.

Rambeau was as noble in spirit as he was in body. Always a loving and friendly gentleman, he was a fine specimen, and his mark on our flock remained for generations. After many good years of producing champions, a bit of us went with him into a special place in the pasture under some spruce frees. When subzero weather occurs, I can see his big, snowy-white head with its Roman nose, alert ears, and great dark eyes as he hung it between our shoulders while riding peacefully to a new home and destiny.

Memory of a Perfect Winter Day

Decades ago, the American pianist George Winston recorded a beautiful solo, "January Stars." A few oft-repeated notes and its flowing chords seem to bring forth a true vision of a star pierced sky.

Winter brings its trials, but stars never seem to be so magical, brilliant, and abundant as in their full sweep of a cold winter sky. There is that treasured moment before bedtime to step out into frigid air for a long look at the lanterns of Heaven and a moon caught in a pine filter. Its shadow tones over the iced silk of snow, silvering the night.

Our New Year's evening of 1984 began with stars. By morning there was a powerful Nor'easter that raged through most of the day. When it began to wane in the late afternoon, Jim and I spent two hours on the spindrift-covered shore of Pemaquid Point. The storm was still bringing tons of lead-gray sea water crashing onto the craggy, stone-jawed ledges, whose foaming waterfalls from the previous wave never finished pouring off before becoming drowned again.

Although there had been many people to share this splendor with throughout the day, at this later hour we were completely alone on that long stretch of ragged rock and violent tumbling of stone, surging breakers, and wild, salt-laden wind. So might two people feel, as we did, that they were just discovering a new world, overpowering in the force of its elements—alone but strong, wanting to stay and challenge this fearsome and glorious clash between sea and shore with the defiance that has always been man's primal response to nature.

The wind is cold but sweet, the salt spray sharp and delicious. The body is nearly numb with the misted blasting of wet surf, but how can we leave now just when the biggest seas yet are pounding in translucent aqua under their massive curving tops? The show is far from over, but passion wanes with chill, falling darkness, and thoughts of dry clothes and the fireplace. Although they will have a few more scars, we know the battle of wind and sea with the shore will again be won by the stoic spruce and granite. Climbing our way back to the truck, we had the deeply satisfying feeling that has recurred so often through the years: Where else could we live so happily among fine neighbors and yet be free enough to be completely alone on one of the most beautiful stretches of coast in the world during one of its splendid upheavals?

The next day, the cobalt-blue sea smiled lazily in the pale winter sun as though it had not been a roaring tyrant just the day before. Instead of being yesterday's discoverers of a savagely beautiful new planet, we were eagerly awaited by some very domesticated woolies who wanted their breakfast of Bristol hay.

CHRISTMAS MIRACLE

November brought us up short against the wall of winter reality. We ask, "Snow now?" "Power outages already?" "What happened to fall?" The calendar doesn't agree, but winter has arrived, so time to lean in and know that living in Maine is worth every day of it.

Christmas is almost here. Snow has been forecast since October and, like every fast-moving seasonal change, it will soon be upon us. Early winter helps to put us in the mood. It also reminds me of one of my favorite Christmas stories.

One year during our fifty-eight years of managing Blue Hill Fair's sheep dog trials, one of the border collie handlers named Bill told us all of an experience he once had. Bill is a tall, gentle fellow. His beard is red-gold, as is his long, wavy hair. When working his dogs, he keeps his hair in a ponytail. Bill, his sheep, and his border collies live on Cape Cod.

One early dawn of the day before Christmas, Bill was awakened by a phone call from the local police. They asked him to bring a dog with all possible speed to a nursing home some distance away, as they had a very difficult situation. A flock of sheep had broken through a fence, disrupted traffic on a major highway for a long distance, and were presently milling around the lawns of a nursing home.

The police promised to meet Bill there to clear traffic so he and his dog could herd the sheep back up the road to the farm they had escaped from. Bill leaped out of bed, didn't bother with a ponytail, wrapped a long white robe over his pajamas, whistled for one of his dogs, grabbed a shepherd's crook, jumped into his truck, his dog beside him, and headed for the nursing home.

Bill soon had the flock rounded up into a group, the dog circling to keep them under control. As he stood with the sheep and waited for the police to clear traffic, he noticed that the nursing home residents were staring out the windows with awestruck expressions. So were the people in stopped cars. Many were looking with reverence at this sight. A few of the nursing home residents were making the sign of the cross. Bill, who was just doing what he does best, wondered at the unusual attention until he began to realize that as he stood there in his white robe, holding the shepherd's crook upright, his long hair and beard blowing gently in the wind, surrounded by sheep on this day before Christmas, that these good people may have been thinking the Second Coming had begun.

Look Under the Bed

Animals. How different life would be without them. The food source aspect is obvious and strictly practical. What compels the stirring of our hearts is their beauty, honesty, comedy, affection, often love, and truth of character. Life without the presence of animals is beyond my imagination. I smile each day at the bleating of sheep, the foghorn bellow of cows, geese whose *squonk* is like a raspberry call during a bad play, the ducks' nasal quacking, and the incessant gossip of hens, occasionally silenced by the royal trumpet of Caesar, the majestic rooster.

Then there is the thrill of the wild animals—a lordly bull moose meandering through the sheep pasture, a cow moose and her calf in the hayfield on a frosty April morning, deer coming to drink at the farm pond not even disturbing the mallards or the great blue heron who stalks its edges in slow motion.

Most of us have heart-tugging memories of many pets through the years; dogs and cats, each unique and beloved. All of ours shared our bed, a border collie usually at our feet and kitties around our heads. The marmalades, black onyx, blazing hues of the tri-colors, creamy coffee of Siamese. We fell asleep to dog snores, purrings that rumbled in baritone, rusty grinding, or smooth humming. Soothing bonds of love and peaceful comfort.

There is a story to each pet. One that surfaces for us often is about an elderly couple, John and Mary, we met during a brief stay at a Florida Keys campground. The Keys have many feral cats. Neutering is sadly neglected, and kittens are profuse. A large number of these sad little creatures lived in that campground, rummaging through garbage and fearfully looking for hand-outs. We put food out at our site, but could never get near the kittens.

John and Mary had been in the campground all winter and had successfully fed a kitten to "teenage" level and tamed it enough to be able to touch it. They had three cats and a dog of their own with them, and when they left in spring they were determined not to leave the little feral cat behind. They caught it easily, put it in their RV with the rest of the pet family, and started their spring trip home to Michigan. On their first night out they opted for the spacious quarters of a motel and chose one that offered a ground floor room with an outside entrance directly into it. This choice was based on being able to sneak the animal family into the room. All sanitary pet supplies were also brought in. The night was smooth and restful and after breakfast John and Mary pulled the drapes on the entire end wall of ceiling-to-floor glass and let the sun shine in.

Baggage was loaded into the RV and the pets were next. The dog and three kitties came promptly for the loading call, but the fourth, the Keys kitty, was nowhere to be found. John and Mary knew it had not escaped, as door openings had been very careful. They checked every possible place a cat could hide—bathroom, behind and in furniture, and under the bed. No kitty. Anywhere. Perplexed and anxious, John took another close look under the bed and saw that there was a torn hole in the fabric that covered the bottom of the box spring. He reasoned that KK (as they had named him) had probably climbed through the hole and was hiding out in the box spring.

John and Mary were dressed in their traveling clothes and shoes and all was ready for the trip, but they couldn't leave without KK. John soon devised the only way to get the kitten out. He and Mary climbed up on the bed and began vigorously jumping up and down all over the bed's surface. Although elderly, they were spry and gave this effort all they had. For the sake of balance on the springy bed, they joined hands and did high leaps in a big circle, Ring-around-the-Rosie fashion. So intent were they that it was awhile before they looked at the huge window-wall and saw the motel room cleaning attendant leaning on her service cart completely absorbed in watching two old people cavorting on the bed like happy children.

At that moment they saw KK flash out from under the bed and head for the bathroom where he was easily caught. They waited until the lady with the cart had decided the show was over and moved on before they rushed out to the RV with KK firmly in hand. John and Mary wrote us about this adventure sometime later. They had KK neutered and he is now a loving member of their household. Every rescue counts.

Sun Moods

When a late January's day of driving rain filled the narrow stream behind the house, I spent soothing, dreaming moments just watching it slide through its winding banks past the owl tree, the barred owl's favorite perch at twilight. The waters silently pooled on the Sheepscot River and ultimate destiny of the sea.

There is a riveting beauty in moving water, whether it is a small stream reflecting a skyline of pines or ocean breakers pouring off a stone-jawed ledge. Sunlight is also a source of moods. As a child I used to think of sunlight always being the same until I became aware of the sun's seasonal character. So bright in summer, crisp gold in September, thin wash of pale light in winter, soft warmth in spring.

Sunshine and happy thoughts are supposed to be synonymous. But sometimes I find them inexplicably sad. In the brilliant splendor of an August day when the sky is a heart-shaking blue and sunlight dominates every plane of rock, tree, and cloud, a strange little tendril of melancholy unfurls within me. Is it because this is the pinnacle of a perfect day and it will soon be gone?

I thought back to the winter months of long ago when we had a large flock of sheep. During afternoon chore time in the barn, the sun slanted through the spruce trees and the open southwestern side of the sheep barn to lay a wan gilt light on the hay cribs. A few spears of hay were highlighted as well as the edges of the cribs' wood structures which were worn smooth, oiled, and waxed by the lanolin of reaching necks. Even the eyelashes of the ewes were turned to gold as they nuzzled the fragrant dried grasses of summer.

Why should a pale splash of sun on this peaceful scene bring a touch of wistfulness? Perhaps it was the thought of the many hundreds of lambs born in the barn over the years, the patina of the hay cribs and grain feeders sending the message of passing time.

The feeling was elusive. I couldn't put a name to it.

Paintings of simple scenes may not have become great, or any meaning as deep, if it were not for the angle of light the artist used. Sun and shadows create similar tender portraits in nature, but they are fleeting, viewed again only in memory.

Recollections of Winter 1971

When we live where there are four seasons, we are inclined to compare each one with those of previous years. There are always a few that stay in memory. As I look through the felted gray fog of our February days, I think of a February several decades ago. From its first day, there was no precipitation of any kind until very late summer. It was a long and delightful spring until the extended drought caused hardship in many ways.

Then there was the winter of 1971, and the snowfall total of 125 inches. Following are some of the notes I kept during that winter on the sheep farm.

Weather continues to be the all consuming subject. It has become the pivot on which we revolve daily here on the farm. Wrapped in layers of woolens and ancient cast-off fur pieces, we waddle from sheep barn to chicken barns armed with ice picks, portable heaters, hammers, screwdrivers—any tool is fair game if it will cause the water systems to yield a supply or separate ice from buckets and water tubs. Night temperatures have been minus zero for so long now I half expect to see a glacier appearing on the horizon soon.

Our usual January Chinook did arrive in the form of a couple of days of balmy forty degrees, but it was accompanied by lashing rain. The snow was barely lowered, and any water remaining on the paths and driveway turned to vast ice areas when the thermometer plunged to its favorite minus zero mark once more.

Now before we could start chipping ice to provide water for the animals, we had to get the barn doors free of their frozen base. With so much snow on the ground, the rainwater couldn't drain off and found every inconvenient place to hide and freeze.

The farm animals calmly adjust to whatever nature offers and greet us with unfailing enthusiasm at chore times. The sheep, encased in their heavy fleeces, are equally happy with their choices of lying on the frozen snow mountains out in their corral or on straw bedding inside the barn.

The ducks rush for their cracked corn with soft, throaty quacks, squatting to warm their bright orange paddle feet while scooping corn with their shovel faces. The geese, loud and imperious, have to be lured to another dining spot to keep peace in the water bird family.

Julie, the long-eared Nubian goat, applies herself to sun soaking with a singleness of purpose. She perhaps wonders which of her wandering ancestors to blame for her ultimate displacement from the warm African deserts.

Winter nighttime in the barn is a place of peace and inspiration, an insight into the kindness and sharing that animals are capable of. The sheep lay about chewing their cuds or sleeping. The two pigs, Samson and Delilah, have made a tunnel under their gate, and they use it at night to join the sheep so they can snuggle tightly against the warm fleeces. Ducks squat on the backs of the sheep, their feet deeply sunken into the comforting wool. The sheep accept these nocturnal companions with a parental attitude. It is part of sharing life on the farm.

The battles of winter seem long until in late February, there is a subtle change in afternoon light, a message that spring is making its way north to Maine. Visions come to mind of birch branches soon turning to a lavender network, the primal pungency of wet dark earth and tree bark, snow melt, and mud under foot. Then comes pure, piercing bird song along with the March hill, the last phase of winter.

Dad's Wooden Ice Skates

In later years, so many questions about our parents' childhoods come to mind that we wish we had asked when they were still here to tell us about their early lives. We remember many tales, but we want to hear more. In my youth I thought Mother and Dad would always be here. Later, daily life gets caught up in so many time-consuming changes that we think, "Someday, I'll have to ask about that." Then all at once, it is too late. What I do remember of my father's childhood stories helps me to picture the settings of the family farm he was born on in Lithuania in the year 1895.

Dad was the oldest of four brothers and two sisters. His father's income as the local sheriff was limited, but in those times all families provided their own food production from farming—cows, chickens, sheep, pigs, grains, and large gardens. Dad learned how to grow anything that could be planted and how to extend the use of all the farm produced in every form.

There were draft horses, but no power equipment. Hay was mowed with scythes and stored loosely in the barns. Wheat and oats were pulled and secured into stooks. Actual whole foods provided all meals—vegetables, grains, raw milk. Dad was a strong, healthy man and had every one of his white teeth when he passed away at ninety-four years old. The family raised their own wheat, and my father sometimes made cereal the way he had done at home, soaking whole wheat kernels overnight and cooking them in the morning until the grains burst. The flavor was soul-satisfying. So was the whole wheat bread he made when Mother gave him some kitchen time.

Cutting hay with scythes was hot, heavy work and Dad's family had a switchel recipe of their own. I'm not sure of all that was in it—probably some vinegar, water, and no doubt at least a smattering (or more) of vodka. One of Dad's tales was about a burning hot day when this drink was sorely needed. The neighboring farmers pitched in to help each other with haying, and on this day one of them gave in to a short nap while propped against a shade tree. The others in the haying crew thought it would be a fine idea to place a good chunk of a cowpie on the fellow's chest. The heat and the switchel had him sleeping peacefully, but as the cowpie began exuding its heavy scent of manure, the neighbor, with eyes still closed, mumbled, "Mamma! Take the kids away!" Dad always laughed heartily when he related this.

Like all self-supporting farms, work hours were long and hard for all family members, but there was fun to be had as well. Dad and his siblings learned to swim by being thrown into the lake by older family members who believed the children's survival instincts would bring them safely to shore. My dad was a powerful swimmer.

Skating in winter was a fine sport, but Dad's time spent at it was severely shortened by the fact that his skates were carved from wood and strapped to his boots. The wooden blades were well-shaped for skating, but they soon absorbed moisture from the ice and would no longer slide. A few families were able to buy steel strap-on skates for their children and Dad badly wanted a pair. One day he asked his grandfather if there was a chance of such a possibility. His grandfather suggested that Dad's best solution would be to put his thumb in a certain area and skate on his elbow.

March and the Mud

March mud is different from mere surface mud and shallow puddles. It isn't just driveways and dirt roads that cause one's feet to disappear. Stepping onto an innocent looking lawn can bring on ankle submersion. Three feet of frost is leaving the ground. Having taken up residence on this earth in a time when all town roads in Bremen and Bristol were dirt and single track, I remember very well how March mud changed our lifestyle in early spring.

My parent's car stayed in the barn, only to be taken out for a trip to Damariscotta or Waldoboro early in the morning if the ground had frozen overnight. The Shore Road in Bremen was typical of most. It was a morass, a bog waiting to swallow anything that entered it. Those that did venture either had to bring a team of horses to get hauled out (not always successful) or remain sunk to the axles until late April's drying winds and sunshine came along.

My father taught me to drive on this road in mud season. Staying out of the ruts and the ditches was an exhilarating challenge, and I loved it. Now it is a skill I no longer need. Every season has its joy, and my March mud joy was school being closed, sometimes for nearly six weeks, because of roads that weren't passable even with the loads of rock and hay that were dumped in the worst spots.

I was free to roam the ever fascinating shore of Greenland Cove. I dug clams among the ice cakes and pulled snails from the ledges for my cat Smudgie who followed me as I gathered them. Then up the hill to the kitchen where I cooked them for him. I picked them out with a darning needle (we darned socks in those days!) then watched his delight as he settled on his haunches all slit-eyed and contented with his favorite meal.

Behind my childhood home, there was a great forest of tall pines. The silken whisper of their needles kindled many beautiful imaginings as I wandered in the depths of that magical place. Even as a child, there was the awareness of the clean purity of the woods and the comfort of its loneliness.

March is the poor, bedraggled end of winter. Roadside snow is dirty. Now that roads are paved, frost heaves and hollows make driving a spring sport as items from the back seat fly to the front. Lawns are adorned with broken branches and there is a mist of melting snow, the demise of a season. But in early mornings there are maple sap icicles to be savored —broken from the branch, cold and sweet. Sun holds a promising warmth, spring and summer birds are arriving. Maine spring is our reward for the long winter and March mud.

We live here because Maine is clean sky, ocean, wild flowers, dark fir and spruce, and always the scent of pine and sea. Salt and sea roses. No other place matters when all this is home.

FLIGHT FROM THE BUMBLEBEE

The truth is the flight was from honeybees, not the noble creature of that great piece of music "Flight of the Bumblebee." My thoughts had wandered to spring, as they do in winter, perhaps because it seems to be the season we yearn for most. Bird calls and the silvery music of peep frogs break the winter silence. Tender air carries the primal scent of earth, and it awakens our instinct to dig and plant.

My father had such a magic touch for growing things that I almost believed he could make anything break through the earth, fat and fruit laden, just by making a secret gesture over his gardens. As my husband said, "No weed would dare show its face." Dad actually strove diligently at all his farming projects, with considerable help from the fertilizer his cherished cows produced.

A favorite endeavor of Dad's was his honeybees. He managed them so well and with such caring attention that he was rarely stung. This made him confident they would not sting my mother when he asked her to watch the process of removing honeycomb. The beehives were kept under a huge pine tree located in pastures thick with clovers and wild flowers. Nearby a watering hole for the cows had formed in a wide area of a small stream.

On this sun-drenched day of honey harvesting, my mother stood by in fascination as Dad opened a hive and began removing the honey combs. The bees were not in a good mood and seemed not to appreciate this raid on their hard work. Even the gentle puffs from the smoker

43

can were not calming. It appeared that my mother's presence made them distrustful and they attempted to attack her in force.

My father was big and gentle but also fit, powerful, and swift. My mother was a tiny, slender woman. Dad scooped her up and ran with her to the cow watering hole. The cows had trampled the approach into a wonderful wallow of soft, gooey mud. Although Mother was sputtering protests, Dad rolled her in the mud until only her snapping brown eyes were visible. When he was sure the mud had rid her of bees and all possible pain, he washed her thoroughly in the clear stream. His swift action saved her from any but mild consequences.

We lived at the edge of Greenland Cove in Bremen, and the shoreline was one of my favorite places to explore. I was around ten years old and returning from the shore when I met up with Mother and Dad coming through the pasture gate. Although it wasn't necessary, Dad was carrying Mother because he loved picking her up. They were both laughing at their adventure and told me all the details as we made our way up the hill to the small inn that was home. The following day, the bees gave in quietly and we were assured of honey on Mother's homemade bread the next winter.

Shakin' Down the Acorns

Somewhere in the past I've heard sprightly music with that title. For many decades we lived for a short while each year with acorns shakin' down. For fifty-nine years we showed our sheep at the Fryeburg Fair. Our camper was parked under a big, beautiful oak tree that we have watched grow from its sapling stage. The great spreading branches shed their fall harvest whenever a breeze drifts through. From the oak's heights, the acorns hit the metal roof of our camper trailer with sharp reports like that of small rocks being thrown on its surface. They roll in little diminishing bounces similar to stones being skipped over water. This has become a Fryeburg Fair sound, making us smile as we remember the decades of this unique accompaniment to our nightly sleep.

The amounts of acorns vary from year to year. Sometimes there have been so many we gathered them to take home to our gray squirrel residents, since most of our home forest is evergreen. Squirrels come to the Fryeburg oak in this season of winter food storage to find and hide their prizes. There is plenty for all, but often two squirrels have a spirited contest over rights to the oak and swirl around the tree nose-to-tail in a blurry gray spiral.

The finest part of so many years of showing sheep at the fairs is the old and binding friendships with the livestock families. The fabrics of our lives have been woven together with memories and experiences shared as family generations grow. All of it is more poignant with the inexorable passage of time.

It takes at least three days for the livestock area of a fair to generate its haunting essence of hay, sawdust, and manure. Earthy. Primitive. Real. The symbol of peaceful creatures that provide so much for us all. The food products of the cows, fiber of sheep, the early building of the land by oxen so necessary to our settlers.

Now oxen appear more for exhibit and to show their skills and strength at pulling a load, although many teams still work in the woods twitching logs out to a road.

Watching them is a fine history lesson for those who can't otherwise imagine how the land was cleared, plowed, and harvested before tractors and machinery existed. Draft horses certainly played a great role as well, but oxen were an economical by-product of the cows kept by the settlers.

In all our years of showing sheep at agricultural fairs, I have to say we have never seen an ox being abused, and we have been in the background of all animal activity. Raising and training oxen is a great Maine tradition. It is heartwarming to see elderly couples with their teams, lovingly caring for their sleek, well-fed animals who respond to them with gentle affection. Many of these couples have grandchildren training teams of calves who follow them only with the waving of a stick and voice commands. What a very real way for young people to learn responsibility and respect for animals—and for themselves as well.

Fryeburg Fair always seems to end too quickly. Our livestock community of animal varieties is a small world in itself that is formed for events of competition, hard work, friendships, and laughter. When we come home, it is consoling to have the same barn fragrance of sheep and cattle.

The ewe flock of sheep and their stud ram come running in from the pasture to watch the show sheep being unloaded from the stock trailer along with champion ribbons and Premier Breeder and

Exhibitor awards. The ribbon recipients couldn't care less. They have been petted all day by crowds of people passing through at the fair. Now they are out of their pens and headed for pasture in a wild abandon of leaps and gambols to join their family. The stud ram thinks these lovely maidens are his special gift and comes galloping up to them, ears forward, eyes brilliant and his upper lip curled up over his nose in the comically endearing way of rams and bulls when they perceive the chance of a new romance. There should be a good crop of spring lambs!

Kooni, the Maine Coon cat, rolls around our feet in ecstatic welcome, enjoying a tummy rubbing and spreading the toes of his huge satin-puff paws. Fryeburg Fair was the last of the season. The farm and its family are ready for winter.

Magic in a Mangrove Jungle

On our camping trips to Florida, Key Largo was usually our destination. An inflatable dinghy with a small outboard motor traveled with us. On one calm day we packed a cooler, boarded the dinghy, and headed down the bay and into the mangrove jungles for a day of exploring. The dinghy could get through the small winding channels of this strange, tangled growth, and we proceeded to a hurricane hole we'd heard of. This was a large pond located deep in the mangroves where smaller boats took refuge in bad storms.

As we came to the entrance of this labyrinth we were astonished to find an old, sixty-five foot, and mast-less schooner tied to the mangroves in several directions. The lines that secured her were as old and gray as the boat. It appeared to be deserted until we saw a frail sailing dinghy tied to the stern.

We were compelled to stop and view this once proud vessel that was now adorned from bowsprit to stern with a five-foot layer of everything that had floated past in the last ten years. Old buckets, bits of dinghies, fenders, anything that wouldn't sink was piled high on her decks. Palmetto bugs the size of small mice crawled up the hull and over the piled junk. Our understanding was that in Florida, palmetto bug is just a nice term for cockroach.

Not wanting to get close enough for any to join us, we were about to leave when an old gentleman with fading red hair appeared on the deck and waved to us. It was worth a few cockroaches to talk with him. He was thin, shy, and spoke with a stutter. After asking us where we came from and learning we were from Maine, he was delighted. His name was Red Brown, and he was a Mainer also.

Red's story was fascinating. He was a captain on the last of the sailing schooners and had been around the world many times. In later years he began building the vessel he was on, but bad times came along and he was never able to finish her completely. The boat was, and had been, his home for many years. It was belayed into the mangroves because it couldn't be taxed there, although Red feared that would change.

He lived off of his Social Security, taking his small sailing dinghy into Key Largo to cash his check and buy what few groceries he could afford. He went ashore twice a month, mostly for fresh water. With no refrigeration, he lived on canned food and fish he caught from the boat. He said these were getting scarce. Red was in his high eighties, content with his simple life and rich memories. He became one of our poignant memories.

We moved on through the dark tunnels of mangrove. This plant has created much of the land in the Keys, catching leaves and materials, which over the years become soil, in its high roots. It would be utterly impossible to walk into this web of roots that stand at least two feet up out of the salt water.

The mysterious greenish light of the tunnel opened into a big pond and we shut down the small outboard to drift in the still water, eat lunch, and dreamily observe. Although they seem to be too awkward and flat-footed to be roosting birds, groups of pelicans relaxed on the higher mangroves. They are somewhat comical in appearance, with bright, knowing eyes close together above their giant bills. Add a pair of spectacles and they would look like wise old professors staring down their noses in expectation of an informed answer from a student.

As I tucked leftovers into the cooler, Jim saw two big circles in the water about forty yards away, then two heads. It was a mother manatee and her calf. They disappeared quickly. We kept watching eagerly in that direction, hoping to see them again. Silent stillness for minutes, then suddenly a *woosh* alongside our dinghy and a massive head was resting upon the gunwale regarding us intently. It was the most beautiful yet homely face we'd ever seen—gray with huge, blubbery chops, small but kindly eyes outlined by black, spiky lashes, sagging eyebrows of blubber and black whisker bristles.

The look the manatee was giving us was a sincere invitation to touch her. We reached over and scratched her head gently. She rolled it slightly while we did this for a few moments, then she slid beneath the surface. We sadly decided she had gone. The dinghy rocked slightly, and then she was lying full length against our small boat. The boat was twelve feet long and she was at least fifteen feet in length.

She gave us another inviting look, and we began scratching her back. She rolled side to side in delight but we couldn't reach her full length, so Jim used an oar to lightly pass it up and down her back while I worked on my reachable half. Near her tail were old but deep circular scars where she had been hit by a boat's propeller.

After about ten minutes, the cow manatee dove under the dinghy and came up against its other side. We remarked later she could have turned us upside down in this move, but she seemed to know to dive deeply. She was snuggled against the gunwale, this time with her tummy up. She wanted that scratched also. We happily obliged with oar and hands. She closed her small, dark eyes, folded her flippers over her chest, and sighed audibly. There were no claws on her flippers, just little round button-type nails similar to ours. Manatees are vegetarians.

We spent at least half an hour with this enchanting creature before she dove away to find her calf who was too shy to approach.

This was an experience almost reverent in its quality. It was a time of pure magic to have a huge wild animal trusting enough to allow us to touch her in affection. That lovely manatee emanated a gentle spirit.

When we returned to the campground and recited our manatee adventure, we were told that it is against the law to be friendly with manatees because it encourages them to approach boats. We hadn't known of this rule and were so captivated by our encounter that the thought never occurred to us. We saw absolute sense to the law and never repeated that memorable interlude.

Night on a Fish Carrier

The love of boats can probably come at any time in life. It came to me before actual memory. I was born and raised at Greenland Cove in Bremen and I can't remember a time before I was rowing a dory. My palms had permanent calluses from the oars. The dory was only thirteen feet and not hard to handle.

The first time I ever slept on a boat was with my dad on Gene Leland's *Sardinia*. She was a big, robust, and powerful fish carrier, also called a smack. Gene left her anchored in Greenland Cove for days at a time during sardine and herring season. Seining for tons of these fish took place there through the years. It was an ideal cove for tying off the seines from side to side of the opposing shores. My father sometimes helped the crew haul in the nets full of fish, and we always watched over the *Sardinia* when she was alone in the cove.

At twelve years old, I just had to know what it was like to sleep on a boat. I pestered my dad until he gave in and took up Gene's offer to stay on the *Sardinia* any time we wanted. Mother loved the sea and small boats, but rolling at anchor didn't agree with her equilibrium. After supper, Dad and I took our dory and a pillow and blanket each and rowed out to the big boat. Dad chose the bottom berth, and I was happy with the upper one.

Years of carrying fish left a powerful aroma of *Sardinia*'s cargoes, but it was part of her and so it was wonderful. I loved the gentle soothing motion of the changing tides and fell asleep quickly with a deep feeling of being where I belonged.

Around midnight, I heard a loud and lusty oath from Dad, who had forgotten how tight the space was for him under my berth. He had risen slightly to turn over and received a mighty smack on his head from a crossmember beam above him. He did some mumbling about why he was out here and not home on his and Mother's feather mattress.

We got up at sunrise, a crimson blaze against the pines. Since it was early spring and the smelts were running, Dad suggested we take the dory to the head of the cove and go up the creek to Rooney's (Arunah Weston's) Brook to catch some smelts for supper.

This was my idea of the perfect start to a day. The tide was coming full and sunrise was melting like molten gold on the placid creek waters. We laughed as we leapt around in the brook, catching the smelts by hand. Soon we had a nice mess to take home.

Mother greeted us with her loving smile and a noble breakfast of home-raised eggs and bacon. It was a night and morning to wear on my heart forever like a diamond.

UNCLE ANGUS AND NEWFIE

Thinking back to the days of Greenland Cove and my parent's farmhouse inn, Mayfair House, I have mentioned that many of the inn's guests had stories to tell. One Canadian couple often vacationed late in the season and became close friends with my parents. Following is one of their stories I remember with a smile.

The subject of our conversation was about how in our youth we become easily embarrassed by situations that we will later learn have no importance. Bruce was the name of the gentleman who told of an event which occurred when he was in his teens. Bruce's parents brought him up to respect, honor, and help his elders. One of them he especially had to help at times was his well-aged, eccentric Uncle Angus.

Except for his dog companion, Angus had always lived alone. He was well-educated, opinionated, and demanding. Angus wore severely ragged clothes because he liked them that way. He had a car nearly as old as himself, but failing eyesight kept him from driving it anymore.

One day, Bruce, about nineteen years old at the time, was called upon to take Uncle Angus to the bank. When Bruce arrived, Angus was in the passenger seat of his old flivver and Newfie, his dog, filled the back seat from side to side and to the roof. Angus went nowhere without Newfie. A Newfoundland dog is a noble and magnificent creature, but Newfie was only half Newfoundland. Although he had the wonderful thick, black coat, he was also half Saint Bernard, which caused him to be a great blundering hulk of a dog. He loved to ride and greeted Bruce exuberantly, shaking the car as Bruce took the driver's seat.

When they reached the bank Bruce parked the car at the bank's front door for Angus' easy access. Newfie was left in the car. Bruce guided his uncle into the bank and they waited in the busy customer lineup area that was formed by stanchions and tape, similar to the banks of today.

As they stood waiting in the long line, they could near Newfie. He loved people, was obsessively devoted to Angus, and felt abandoned in the car. His voice range was equal to his size and his whines were wails, his bark a stentorian roar. He drew attention from the waiting customers. Angus told Bruce to bring Newfie into the bank. It was a hot summer day and young Bruce was already embarrassed by his uncle's wool hat with its long tail, his heavy overcoat that was torn and greasy, and his scuffed shoes with no laces.

Angus' old clothes had absorbed many odors over the years and they were now emanating in profusion. Bruce could not see how admitting Newfie into the scene could improve things, and he protested mildly by saying they should soon be done with the banking work.

Uncle Angus fixed Bruce with an icy stare from beneath his bushy white brows and said firmly, "Bring. The. Dog. In." Bruce obeyed.

Newfie was ecstatic and came leaping into the bank with the grace of a cow. His eyes were bright, mouth parted in a huge smile with drool flying. Bruce was in the rear hanging on to the leash, his feet touching the floor only occasionally.

Newfie wanted to be with his master, but Angus directed Bruce to tie the leash to a nearby supporting column as he needed Bruce to help him identify some paperwork. Newfie was not happy with the arrangement, and in his pacing he managed to reach and knock over a couple of the stanchions that supported the customer line-up tape.

This caused a domino effect and the entire thing collapsed around the customers, entangling them in tape and stanchions. Most were annoyed. A few laughed.

Watching their struggles, Newfie thought this looked like great fun and wanted to join in. Since he had the power of a young bull, a couple of lunges at the end of his aging leash freed him to enter the mayhem. He introduced himself to everybody by licking faces and liberally dispensing slobber as the people attempted to extricate themselves from their confinement. A few tellers waiting for customers to free themselves were watching avidly.

Newfie spied new faces for his affections and rushed over to the tellers' area. Smoking in the bank was allowed in those days, and there was a full ashtray at each teller's station. The counters were polished granite and as Newfie put his great paws on them so he could reach the tellers, his feet slid into an ashtray, sending it down the long counters into a few more ashtrays, all of which flew off onto the floor spilling their contents for a good distance.

Bruce, red-faced and sweating, horrified with humiliation, was sputtering apologies as he helped to get people clear of the tape and stanchions. Angus calmly proceeded to the nearest teller and commanded Newfie to join him. But Newfie was busy slobbering over the custodians who had appeared to sweep up the ashtray mess and restore the lineup system.

Chuckling, Bruce said to us, "I'd never had so much of the wrong kind of attention in my life. I can laugh about it now, but it was far from funny to me then. It never bothered Uncle Angus. Newfie could do no wrong!" Smiling reflectively, Bruce continued, "We always thought Uncle Angus was quite poor because of the Spartan way he lived, but he actually was pretty well off, and years later when he passed on to join Newfie, he left me a nice little start in life."

Moonlight and Cabbages

An advantage of passing years is the collection of good memories that come forth to be reviewed with nostalgic pleasure. So many are from Jim's and my six decades on our North Country farm. Sheep were the primary residents of the barn, but farms have a way of gathering many species.

A burro, Hereford cow, ducks, geese, bantam chickens, pigs, a Nubian goat, cats, and a rabbit also lived in the barn, the corral, and some in the farm pond. All of them contributed a special joy to our days. There are stories about all of them and their individual antics. Daffy the rabbit comes to mind.

Daffy's parentage was Giant Checker. He was a large, white rabbit with a black stripe down his back, scattered black spots, black ears, and very dark eyes. Most endearing was the badge of his breed, a perfect black butterfly spread across his twinkling nose and velvet fur chops. A family moving away gave Daffy to us along with the large cage he had been living in.

Fearful of foxes, we kept Daffy in his cage, which was next to the hay pile in the barn. He seemed content in the cage, but shortly after his arrival the spring days were so beguiling we decided to let him try freedom to see if he could manage it safely. At first he stayed within close radius of the sheep barn. He returned at night and patiently allowed himself to be picked up and put in his cage for night safety. One night we were bringing in the day's hay harvest long after dark and found him asleep beside his cage. He couldn't get into it himself and grew sleepy waiting for us.

From that point we no longer confined him. He was a clever, affectionate little gentleman, and nightfall always found him safely settled in the great pile of hay bales.

But one night when a full moon was at its glorious best, we spied him having a midnight snack. He was sitting among the cabbages in the blue-shadowed garden munching happily. Perhaps he was moonstruck, for every few minutes he would spring straight upward into the air, then land in his same spot, appearing to express his joy with a cabbage feast in the midst of moonlight magic.

We never knew where he spent his days, although one afternoon I saw him in the spruce woods that border the farm pond. He was running in the zigzag fashion of rabbits who seem to know that predators can seldom match. Except for his moonlight cabbage repast, we would see him passing the gardens morning and night without touching the vegetables. As he came home, his countenance and bearing seemed bright with the delights of his adventurous day, and he would squeeze through the pasture fence and take a shortcut across the corral. One evening, as he poked his head through the fence, he found a ewe regarding him nose to nose. Daffy was not timid and exchanged sniffs with her, nibbling gently on the sheep's nose as he explored it. The ewe appeared to enjoy this and held her head still until he continued his journey toward the hay pile.

Daffy was friendly with all the farm family: sheep, cow, burro, pigs, and Nell, the border collie sheep dog. He loved to chase the barn kitties playfully and was only slightly intimidated by a peppery bantam hen. She was blue-black and had a fluffy topknot of feathers that hung about her head and eyes in a fringe. It bounced as she strutted around, making her look like a fussy little gossip in a feathered hat. She would scold Daffy and run after him in long strides, her hat fluttering as she extended her neck in angry clucks. Daffy would hop away in his rabbit zigzag, almost laughing at her when she tired of the chase.

Through the cold winter nights we couldn't see where Daffy nested in the hay pile, but as the bales were removed toward spring we uncovered a labyrinth of tunnels he had made to deeply ensconce himself in warmth and comfort. Daffy was a source of delight for years. He reminded me of the wonderful book *Watership Down*, the haunting story of a group of rabbits. There are very few human characters in the book, and the rabbit world in those pages is so unique I almost resented human intrusion when it did occur.

Spring Cleaning the Hard Way

Our discontent with winter will disappear as we revel in the new life of spring. Now we can tackle spring cleaning, starting with the house, then winter's debris outdoors. There have been many springs in my life, and I've been thinking back to when I was a little girl and how my parents dealt with the rituals of spring.

In 1927, my parents bought a saltwater farm on Bremen's Greenland Cove (I was born in Damariscotta two years later). The house was large, so in addition to farming they opened a small summer inn and named it Mayfair House. It needed extensive work, but mother and dad were hardwired for work.

There was no electricity in that remote area, so when spring cleaning began, it was a monumental task compared to today's methods. There were eight bedrooms in the house and each one had a room-sized carpet. These were taken outdoors on a windy, sunny day and dragged over the lush grass lawn several times until no dust appeared. Then they were hung on heavy lines and pounded with a rug beater.

All floors were scrubbed clean with a brush and lye soap. Windows were washed with vinegar and newspaper. Fresh curtains were pressed with flat irons heated on the wood stove. I learned to help at an early age and loved the laughter of the three of us working together. In all seasons, laundry was washed in a huge tub with scrubbing board and Fels-Naptha soap, then hung on lines behind the cow barn to wave in the sea and pine-scented breeze.

Although I was too small to help, I remember my parents preparing huge vegetable gardens by turning the earth with spading forks. No horses or tractor, just their strength and determination. Both were rugged—my mother was barely one hundred pounds but wiry. Dad was all powerful muscle. They loved working together.

While Dad was planting and caring for gardens and livestock, Mother painted and papered the guest rooms. She loved bright and cheerful colors. Each room had a different flower theme.

The first year Mother applied wallpaper to a room and proudly finished it, neighbors Maud and Asbury came to visit. As Mother told the story, Maud related details of a recent trip she and Asbury had taken to the White Mountains. She talked nonstop about the mountains and their high "attitudes" which affected her sinus problems, but at least Asbury could do some walking after the "cartridge" surgery on his knees. When Maud got into the story of getting their dog "spaded," Mother could wait no longer and took Maud to see the newly papered room.

Maud looked, smiled, and said, "But, my dear, you haven't matched the designs!" In her zeal, mother hadn't noticed that the flowers next to the joining of paper strips were only halves and bits. It all had to be removed. My dad and Asbury happened to appear at this moment of revelation.

After Mother scraped the paper from the walls and began again with her new advice, Dad said he would do a couple of strips to show Mother how it should be done. He made this offer with just a hint of superior male knowledge. Mother retained some of her Scottish fire, and this didn't go over well.

They prepared a big bucket of paste, hung the paper over a support for pasting, then carefully carried it up the ladder to begin placing paper just below the ceiling molding. Dad set the paper strips, nicely matching the patterns. Chortling to mother at his success, he climbed down the ladder and stepped into the very full bucket of paste. Mother was happily rewarded.

My parents operated Mayfair House for forty years. Capacity was fourteen to fifteen guests, many of whom returned for decades because of Mother's homegrown food, and the beautiful surroundings of forest, lake and sea.

Meals were memorable. Breakfasts of eggs from our own hens, bacon raised and smoked on the farm, Mother's special bread slathered with butter provided by Dad's Jersey cows. Prime rib roasting in the oven filled the salt air which was reverently inhaled by the guest sitting around in Adirondack chairs. They watched my dad return from his gardens with baskets of asparagus, peas, or the day's seasonal yield.

I happily fetched lobsters from a lobsterman across the cove by rowing our dory. Dad and I dug clams at low tide. He churned ice cream on Sundays using ice from Webber Lake buried in sawdust and stored in our ice house. He also used cream from the cows.

Vacationers in those times came to sit outside, walk, swim in either lake or saltwater, fish, row boats, and enjoy huge meals that remained in their memories. Guests at Mayfair House formed many heartwarming and long friendships. My childhood and teenage years were a time to be cherished—an education of mind and heart for life's journeys to come.

Maine Spring

The long winter whimpered away into that season so eagerly awaited, so precious in all its phases of renewal and hope. Spring. We know it is here because:

Cardinals and robins sing at sunrise.

The staccato of a woodpecker echoes in the woods.

Turtles sun on the banks of the farm pond. Fish create purling circles in the waters that were recently burnished shields of ice.

Pickup trucks haul brightly colored lobster traps to the shore.

Daffodils and hyacinths brave frosty nights to bring forth their ethereal essence.

Pine boughs seem loftier and needles more full, their silken hush softer in the spring wind. Sunrise casts a warmer bronze over the evergreen tops. Poplar trees bear plush puffs and the small garnets of maple blossoms blush with the rising sap.

White birches are displaying their lavender network of sap-rising branches.

A red squirrel sits at the base of a big spruce near his den between its roots. His tiny feet are folded across his chest as he considers the safest route to the bird feeders. Kooni, the Maine Coon cat, watches him from the window, whiskers and tail twitching, raising his big paddle-paw as if to pounce.

Fingers reach into the garden's dark, rich loam to pull the first stray dandelions and witch grass spears. A walk in the woods yields the tingling taste of a wintergreen berry that survived the winter. The powerful scent of damp earth, almond-sweet forest floor and secret green places reaches upward into each breath taken.

Small streams and brooks move like liquid crystal over mossy rocks. Magenta skunk cabbages unfurl close by. Deeper in the woods there is a small bog. Rising from it is the sound of frogs, not trilling like spring peepers but performing a symphony that seems comprised of muted tambourines and cymbals.

From the shore, gulls call their joyous spring cry and the sea wind washes over us like the water itself—cool and smelling of salt, pine, fir, and the mystery of the ocean's great distances.

Here in Maine we live by the seasons, so sharply defined. But the sea is timeless in its seething currents and tides. This blue vastness on our planet soothes, simplifies and heals.

A lifetime in Maine seeps deeply into the blood, the sorcery of it seasoning and enriching each month of the year.

"Now Hear This!"

As we anticipate the joys of boating season, anecdotes about it come to mind. As it should be, the captain is the captain. But when it comes to pleasure boats, there can be a variety of attitudes concerning the captain's position and how he or she believes it should be portrayed.

During a summer stay at a marina dock, a large sailboat was berthed astern of us. It appeared that her captain was possibly a retired admiral, for he had the bearing of one as well as an emphatic attitude about authority. However, it could only be inflicted on his crew of one—his wife. His daily orders to her were many and they always began with "Now hear this!" She snapped to attention and all but clicked her heels and saluted. The scene was especially excruciating when they cast off from the dock or returned.

Boaters on the docks help each other catch a line or push off in tight spots. This gentleman was having none of it. His wife was going to perform those sea duties. His roars of "Now hear this!" could be heard as they approached the dock, and his orders were so confusing that the poor lady was hopping and stumbling, picking up lines, dropping them for others, and leaping from port to starboard, throwing fenders around as "Admiral" changed his mind about which side of the vessel he wanted to come in on.

One day company arrived to visit Admiral and his wife, their baggage indicating they were all going on a cruise. As they went below deck we heard "Now hear this!" several times as the guests were told where they may sit, stand, or take off their shoes. The guests left, and later returned with bags of groceries in hand. Peeking from the top of one bag were a couple of bottles of wine.

Admiral took one scowling look at the wine bottles and bellowed, "Now hear this! There will be no alcohol aboard this vessel. Return these items to your vehicle!" The humbled guests scuttled off with the wine. The group cast off that afternoon with Admiral bawling his muddled orders to his wife while the guests cowered in the cockpit. They were back early the next day, and the guests did not give a backward look as they hurried up the dock with their baggage.

People have different reactions to boat handling situations. Some are stern and abusive like Admiral, but most take things in stride and with civility. One day, a sailboat docked astern of us. The young couple, who had just bought the boat, were learning how to sail. They were getting ready to leave when the husband instructed his wife to untie lines while he stayed on the boat operating the auxiliary engine. He planned to keep the vessel close to the dock so she could board easily. Jim offered to cast off while they were both aboard, but the husband politely declined, saying they had to learn this exercise themselves. Understandable.

The wife struggled with the lines, but in the couple's efforts to be sure the boat was secure, they had tied many serious knots. There is an old saying: "If you can't tie a knot, tie a lot." The husband quietly said, "No problem, Honey, I'll come on the dock and untie." He did so and she watched him admiringly. All lines were now in the water, and the boat with its running engine was leaving quickly with nobody on board.

They stood slack-jawed as they watched. Jim grabbed one of our long boat hooks and caught a floating line, bringing the boat back close enough for the rest of us to catch the remaining lines. Everybody was smiling, husband and wife were placing no blame on each other, and they sailed away peacefully.

Docking a boat is not like parking a car. Wind, tide, current, experience, and the boat's configuration have much to do with either the captain's relief at not crashing into the dock, another boat, or pride of expertise in spite of all odds.

One fellow with a sleek thirty-foot powerboat slid her neatly into the fuel dock in spite of a brisk wind. He proudly waved off an offer from a dock hand to catch his dock line. He leaped nimbly off the vessel with the line in hand and stooped to cleat her down, but the cleat sped past him. The boat engine was running and this captain had forgotten one vital thing—take her out of gear. Holding the line and running down the dock in the futile effort to hold his boat back, his speed increased until his leaps were Olympic and his heels were reaching for the sky.

When he got to the end of the dock, he had to choose between being towed by the boat or letting go of the line. He let go. The boat proceeded on its own to the next dock where it smacked into another boat, rubbing and nudging it until the wind turned its bow so it could continue down the dock and visit other boats the same way.

A friendly boater zipped over in his inflatable dinghy, picked up the hapless captain, and managed to catch the runaway. On the water, no two days are alike.

The Blueberry Expedition

Another long-term summer guest at Greenland Cove's Mayfair House Inn was an immense Scotsman named Sandy MacFeggans who we referred to as Mac. He was six feet three inches tall and boasted of weighing three hundred and fifty pounds. He truly lived to eat and spent the summer joyfully doing so.

Mac was retired from the British Army in Africa, where he had spent most of his life. To listen to him was to believe he had tamed that continent single-handedly. His tales of African safaris and his battles in the Boer War were endless. I had overheard a guest refer to him as a bore and at my early age took this to mean that his combats in the Boer War were to prove who was the biggest bore. I thought he had surely won.

Mother believed in systems and efficiency, and we were always able to get out of the inn for at least two hours each afternoon. Mother liked to go into the woods when blueberries were in season. Two of the younger lady guests asked to go with her the next time she went. When the right afternoon presented mother invited the two ladies to join her in what she always called a Blueberry Expedition. Mac was on the scene and the word "expedition" caught his attention, perhaps reminding him of a safari. He asked to join and Mother, ever the diplomat, politely agreed. Mac grabbed his trusty pith helmet, which he wore outdoors rain or shine. It was his symbol of the mighty African adventurer.

With a white enamel bucket and small bowls for picking, they all set off up the Shore Road, which was little more than a dirt track through the woods that led to Muscongus. In about a mile and a half they came to what was known as Poquette's Hill, where, due to an earlier forest fire, some fine patches of blueberries grew. The ladies picked berries and Mac wandered off toward the woods in search of more harvest. Food gathering was for women, he thought, and he couldn't bend over anyway.

When the bucket was full of blueberries the ladies went looking for Mac. By the time they found him, they were in the pine woods a long way from the dirt road. It was confusing, but mother had a good sense of direction and started heading east toward the sea and the road. Mac vehemently insisted that she was actually heading west and they would be lost. He made it clear that as a man who had slashed his way through many a jungle, he wished to take charge of this expedition and lead them all properly east, to the road and to safety.

His military bearing was convincing, and against her better judgment mother let him take over. He now had an important mission, his first in years. Bristling with authority, he insisted on carrying the bucket of blueberries for these frail ladies.

After half an hour or so of stumbling through the woods, Mac managed to jam both his massive feet at once under a fallen log. The blueberry bucket left his hands and continued on, scattering its entire contents in front of him as he toppled into them belly first. His white shirt and linen knee length knickers were purple with blueberry juice, and his wire-framed spectacles were twisted. Recovering himself with as much dignity as possible, he clapped his pith helmet back on his head and they proceeded.

Mother realized by now that they were off into a huge territory between the road and Webber Lake. The only way out was onward. Since they were indeed heading west, she knew their best hope was to come out at the lake. So my tiny one hundred-pound mother subtly took the lead. Mac puffed along in the rear drenched in purple juice and sweat. After skirting swamps, fighting through underbrush, and climbing ledges they did come to Webber Lake's southeastern shore.

Mac triumphantly wiped his face and claimed that this was where he had planned to head all along. Mother ignored his further suggestions for what he thought would be a certain shortcut from this point to the road and she kept on going. She knew it was still a rough passage ahead over the high-walled ledges of the lake's lower eastern shore, but that it was the one sure way to our trail home from the lake.

Supper was always served at 6:00 p.m. in the evening. It was now 6:15. Mother was never late with meals, and my Dad was frantic when she had not appeared in the kitchen at her usual time of 5:00. He had walked to the blueberry patch but found no trace of anyone. Knowing the guests were expecting supper, he went to the gardens for lettuce and tomatoes, and I had set the table and shelled out lobster for salad as scheduled. When mother rushed into the kitchen, in her woods-torn overalls and with bits of branches in her hair, she whipped up a batch of cheese biscuits (no blueberry muffins tonight!), Dad and I had lobster salad ready, and all was well, if a little late.

Dressed in fresh white knickers and shirt, Mac sat at the head of the table, the only place he would fit, and with grand flourishes regaled the guests with the tale of how his jungle expertise had just saved three ladies from a night certain to have been spent in the great Maine Woods. The two ladies who had been there snickered quietly.

WALKING THE PLANK

Embarrassing moments. How we are more acutely affected by them in our youth and perceptions of ourselves change. I'll start with mine when I was six years old. I have mentioned my parents small summer inn, Mayfair House, located at Greenland Cove in Bremen. Webber Pond was a short distance through a pine woods at the back of the inn. Our pastures looked out to Hog Island and the Audubon Nature camp.

The Audubon campers had my parent's happy permission to land in our pasture, walk up by the inn, and take the trail to Webber Pond. This gave the groups of twenty or more people a chance to observe plants and insects in the fields, bird life on the mainland and through the woods to the pond, and the varieties of life around the pond, which was actually a lake.

With no children or neighbors nearby, my world was the woods and saltwater shore. I was eager to follow the Audubon groups when they came along every couple of weeks with new guests. Mr. Cruikshank, one of the Audubon's fine leaders and professors, kindly allowed my presence as long as I was completely silent. All participants had to be so that delicate bird calls could be heard and identified and the leader could make comments. Even at this early age, I learned a great deal, mostly because it was all about nature and the place I was happiest.

When the group returned to the farm-inn, Mr. Cruikshank would always ask me to sing a song for them all before they went to the pasture and the waiting boat. Without hesitation, I would climb up on a ledge and belt out "Jingle Bells" with all I had. It was the one piece I knew the words to. I was six years old, freckle-faced, and completely unconcerned by what I know had to be a toneless but loud rendition.

Embarrassment and silly values were not in my awareness then. However, this had changed by the time I was fifteen. At that age, I worked with my parents at the inn from dawn to dusk seven days a week, except for a couple of hours in the afternoons when I went swimming either in Greenland Cove or Webber Pond. One of the duties I especially loved was rowing the thirteen-foot dory across the big cove to lobsterman Leslie Collamore's dock and bringing lobsters back for the inn.

On this day it was early summer and I was wearing my new swim suit for the season—a snug, shiny white latex, popular material back then. Always looking to sneak in a swim if I was near water, I planned on being prepared. At that time there was an older summer cottage next to Leslie's dock. I saw several teenage girls sitting on the rocks looking at magazines, polishing their nails, and looking (I thought) quite sophisticated. I decided they were definitely from the city and probably amused by this country native with braids wrapped around her head helping drag lobsters out of a crate.

When the lobsters were loaded into the dory, I went up to Leslie's camp for the change from the money my folks had sent with me. When I returned to the dock, I realized that because of the receding tide, Leslie had moved my dory to the front edge of his float that I must cross to get to the dory.

The float was old and so waterlogged that it was completely covered with a bright green growth so slippery you could fall down just by looking at it. A strong southwest wind had picked up and was coming into the open cove from Muscongus Bay and the sea. The waves had set the float in motion. Normally in a slippery situation like this I would have eased my way along, arms out, bent over and taking small pigeon-toed steps. Was I going to do that in front of these city girls watching me with obvious amusement? Indeed not! I was a native. I could walk over this stuff, no problem. Head up, I stepped out smartly.

My first step was the end of being upright. I went down like somebody had thrown me from a height. The water was slopping over the float. It was slanting and rolling in the seas, so I knew I would probably slide off into the water. If that happened, I would have to swim back to the dock and tackle the float all over again. Being on my back, I couldn't see anything to grab so I made things worse by turning on my front. In this position, I managed to totally cover myself with heavy green scum from head to foot as I slid helplessly along the float. One big wave came along and threw me into the dory all in a heap.

My face was flaming and my new white swimsuit was poison-green. I dared a sideways glance at the group of girls. They were choking with laughter. Well, why not. Back on the home shore I unloaded the lobster baskets onto the smooth sloping ledges, pulled the dory out on its off-haul, and dove into the water to scrub off the green slime. My suit was green the rest of the summer.

My mother listened to my tale of humiliation and in her Scottish way said, "Aye, well, 'pride goeth before a fall.'" Wasn't that the literal truth! But mother was kind and gentle, my best friend. She hugged me, saying "Never mind, the poor dears will soon have to go back to the city and you'll still be here enjoying everything they have to leave behind." I found myself feeling sorry for the girls.

Embarrassing Rescue

One of my embarrassing moments was walking the plank. Now it's Jim's turn.

Jim and I have been married for fifty-six years at this point and, like any couple united that long, we have been through many different experiences. As we reminisce occasionally about our life's adventures we seem to end up saying: "We've been through a lot together!"

We saw a sign not long ago that we loved. It read, "We have been through a lot together and most of it was your fault!" I'm happy that we can't say that to each other, as all of our decisions have been made mutually.

Jim is a mellow guy with a great sense of humor, so I hope he won't mind me telling this. After all, it's no secret—about two thousand people saw it happen. The event took place in East Boothbay at the launching of a huge sailing yacht named *Antonisa*. She was built by the Hodgdon Brothers and was an impressive vessel that belonged to a gentleman from Italy. A cove in Linekin Bay was the nearest place she could be moved to from her building site. It took a lot of engineering to get her to the shore and it had to be a tidal launching.

There was no space for parking vehicles except for those of the dignitaries involved. All others attending walked to the launch site. Seating was wherever it could be found on grass or rocks around the shore of the cove. We arrived early and settled close to the shore. It was a beautiful day of bright sun and billowing clouds. There had been a heavy storm out at sea a couple of days before, and the cove was covered in a huge blanket of seaweed. It undulated with the incoming tide on the entire surface of the water.

The crowd continued to gather and soon filled the small area. *Antonisa* was awaiting full tide to begin floating, and a narrow platform extended to her bow for the smashing of the champagne bottle. Flags flew, Scottish bagpipers played, speeches were given. The excitement was building by the moment. When *Antonisa* appeared to be responding to the tide, her owner's wife approached with a beribboned bottle. It didn't break until the fourth hard wallop across the vessel's bow.

We had noticed a couple of large square objects the size of crates covered with cloth and kept wondering what they contained. We soon found out. When the champagne bottle had yielded its contents, a man whipped the cloth away from the crates, opened them, and released a dozen white doves. Most flew uncertainly into the air, but four of them fell in the water.

The huge covering of loose, floating seaweed supported three of them enough so they could gain flight again, but the fourth dove floundered helplessly, sinking deeper into the seaweed as it flapped its wings desperately seeking flight. The big crowd watching were loudly and collectively expressing concern about its situation, but none made a move. Jim said, "This isn't going to happen." Without taking time to remove his shoes or roll up his jeans, he waded into the floating seaweed and gently picked the dove out of it just as its head was disappearing. The crowd roared in approval, some yelling out "He saved it!" Then Jim, now well over his knees in water and seaweed, turned toward shore.

Because nothing was visible beneath the floating weed, he lost his footing over a large rock and fell into the water up to his chin. But he held the dove aloft in his right hand while searching under the water with his foot for a purchase to right himself again. The crowd made concerned noises while Jim struggled on.

Soaking, wringing wet, dripping water with seaweed hanging from his elbows and back pockets, Jim delivered the dove safely to its owner. The crowd of about two thousand people clapped. Angus King, Maine's Governor at the time, had made a fine launching speech. He graciously came to Jim and, with a big smile, shook his hand and congratulated him on his efforts to rescue the dove.

Knowing the only course was to carry through in the spirit of the day, Jim thanked Governor King and bowed to the smiling crowd, a few strands of seaweed falling forth as he did. We went up the road laughing together over the comical drama while Jim's clothes dripped and his shoes sloshed.

Mr. Poe and the Ravens

Six decades on our North Country farm provided us with several domestic and wild animal learning experiences as well as the joys and wonders of nature. One story that comes to mind is our observation of a raven. This privilege came about because of our farm ducks. They began laying eggs in large amounts by early March. Usually they deposited them in soft nests near the hay pile or in a hollow spot under the molasses barrel when they had the urge to set. Often they were caught off-schedule and the daily egg would be dropped in the barnyard or on the banks of the pond. A couple of the ducks seldom managed to reach a nest in time, and their eggs landed in the sheep corral daily.

As it occasionally does, March had roared in all fang and claw and sideways winds. On such a day, a large onyx-black raven landed on a fence post. He dropped into the corral next to a few duck eggs. Placing one egg neatly in his big beak, he flew off into the pines with it. He returned shortly for a second egg, which he took to the bank of the farm pond and, holding it carefully between his claws, pecked a hole in it and withdrew the contents for his breakfast. He then made two more egg trips back into the pine woods.

We watched this procedure from the kitchen window using binoculars for several mornings and soon concluded the raven had taken the first egg and the others to his mate after he had eaten his. She did not appear but, thinking of Mr. Poe, we named her Nevermore and the male One More, since he always came back for one more egg for himself after he delivered his mate's. If there was a morning when there was only one egg in the corral, he didn't eat it but obviously took it away to Nevermore. We could hear her greeting him excitedly. Ravens have a loud and distinctive croaking call.

Eventually we put several eggs and some bread slices on a flat stone near the pond when there were no duck egg mishaps in the corral. From these, One More always took Nevermore's breakfast to her before leisurely enjoying his own.

One day we saw One More pulling bits of wool that had collected on the fence as the sheep had rubbed past it through the winter. He patiently got his gathering together in a large mass, then dropped it all as he took off into flight. The raven was graceful in the air, but hopelessly awkward on landing. He hopped in jagged leaps and when he got most of the wool back in his beak, there was still some trailing and he stepped into it, tripping and tilting himself in uncertain directions.

For several days One More collected scraps of wool from the corral fence until there was no more to be found. One early morning, after delivering breakfast to Nevermore, he returned and landed in the sheep corral. Following a fruitless search for wool on the fence, he approached a sleeping sheep in his stumbling fashion. He cocked his head and, regarding the ewe with his bright, black eyes, he hopped up on her back with the aid of his great flapping wings. The ewe woke up and looked around at him but, being accustomed to ducks and lambs sleeping on her back during cold nights, she was not perturbed by One More and began chewing her cud. Sensing her peaceful attitude, the raven settled to his business of the day—providing a luxury nest for Nevermore and their family that was in the process of hatching.

We watched in fascination as he dipped his head into the bulky depths of the ewe's fleece and, bracing his feet, pulled forth big chunks until his beak was filled with bright wool. The sheep continued to chew and lay quietly, never missing this contribution from her abundant coat. One More had to make two heavily laden flights to take away his treasure. We have never forgotten this special scene and still regret that a camera wasn't handy.

As spring unfolded and the ravens' natural food became available, we didn't see One More, but we could hear his and Nevermore's special rusty calls as well as the high clatter of their young. Males of animal and bird species don't always have anything to do with family life beyond mating. It was touching to see One More work diligently to feed his mate while she attended to hatching and to see that her nest was lined with soft, warm wool, some of it fresh from the sheep, no less!

A barnyard society is at its finest and beautiful best when wildlife interacts in peace and harmony with farm animals.

Climbing the Towers

Many people are drawn to the sea either because they were brought up next to it, as it was for Jim and me, or for its endless fascination. Exploring it, making a living from it, enjoying its beauty, challenging its danger, and being awed by its constant change pulls us to its shores. As all surface land water finds its way to the sea, so do most humans at some time in their lives.

There are things unique to the ocean and its coastlines that are found nowhere else, such as lighthouses. People are captivated by them even if they have no experience with boating or realize the importance of their existence.

Lighthouses have always had a meaning for us beyond their value when making a passage on a dark night. As teenagers, we were privileged to have the light keeper at Pemaquid Point take us up inside that wonderful old tower. It was not very high, but history seeped from its walls.

Anywhere we find a lighthouse in our travels we have to see it, walk around it, read about its past, and hope we can be allowed inside. Few are open to the public. One that was open was Cape Hatteras Lighthouse, that massively tall and black spiral striped spire on the Outer Banks in North Carolina. It has rested upon that flat and boundless sandpit for many decades.

A few years ago we climbed two hundred and forty-two steps to its top. On the way we observed with vague concern the many deep, long, darkened cracks in its walls and marveled that the whole thing hadn't given up in a hurricane. It looked ready and waiting for one.

When our weary bones arrived at the top, a uniformed attendant was greeting the breathless who had completed the struggle. He looked to be quite fit and in his forties. I asked him if he made this journey every day, thinking he must be almost able to jog up the great length of steps by now. He replied that he did, and that he dreaded the killing pain of it each day.

The view was far reaching. High surf pounded the interminable miles of sand. There was beauty in it, but also relentless monotony of sand, sea, and horizon unbroken by forested islands like the Maine coast. Going down the steps was almost worse than going up. My legs quickly turned to rubber.

A few years after our visit to Cape Hatteras, when the mammoth task of moving this lighthouse back from the encroaching sea had successfully taken place, we could only think of the tower's great age and the stress cracks in its walls. We marveled at man's ingenuity to ensure its survival of the move.

Our most cherished lighthouse visit took place on our own Maine Coast. The lighthouse is perched on the ledges of a relatively small, thickly spruce-covered island. There must have been a house by the light, but it has been gone for decades. There is no habitation on the island—it is completely wild, likely because landing on it is so difficult. It is all stone-jawed rocks. No coves or small beaches. Perhaps in the days of the light keeper there might have been a crude railway. We couldn't imagine how they off-loaded supplies. With the light now automatic, this was no longer a problem.

As we passed this island, we often wanted to land on it and explore around the lighthouse, the spruce woods, and the shore, but there was always breaking water to deter us. One calm mid-summer day, we were not far from the island and saw there were only smooth swells sweeping the rocks.

We looked at each other with a glance that said *This is the day.*

We dropped the anchor in the lee of another island, lowered the inflatable dinghy, and headed for a long flat ledge near the lighthouse that seemed the most logical place to land. The swells were long, but reasonably gentle enough to negotiate the ledge without tearing the bottom out of the *Rubber Ducky* if we timed the waves carefully. With the dinghy safely above the water line, we set out for the adventure we had been waiting for.

The rock outcroppings around the tower had several indistinguishable, weather-worn initials and dates carved into them. The old dates showed that it had to be the light keepers who labored to put their initials here, perhaps as a way to leave their mark during those long and lonely days.

The island was on its own planet of sun, wildflowers, and pungent aromas of spruce and the sea. Profound silence reigned as well. But, oh, the lighthouse! In delighted awe we saw that its simple rugged door was half open, and there was no latch on it. We hesitantly peeked inside. The iron spiral staircase was heavily rusted, and the walls inside were darkened with age. The ancient past of this edifice was so penetrating we found ourselves whispering in reverence.

As we climbed the rust-encrusted stairway, it shuddered often, and every step we took echoed in a resounding clang. At the top we stood entranced for almost an hour by the astounding view of islands, ocean, and distant mainland. What made it so special was that we were the only two people on the island and in the lighthouse of this small, magical world. When we left, we searched for a large rock and propped it against the tower door so it couldn't blow open anymore. We felt we had been allowed to be part of a beauty so deep and moving it was almost a religious experience.

The Cows are Drunk

Each season brings its own memories. Long-awaited spring takes me back to green fields, and the joys of farm animals first released from their confinement to go out to their pastures and frolic in the sunshine.

Although sheep have been the farm animals of our adult life, I have vivid memories of dairy cows during my childhood on the shores of Greenland Cove. My father kept four milking cows and a replacement heifer or two. Through the years they were mostly Jerseys with sooty, dished-in faces, great fringed soft eyes, and dark honey-colored hides.

With the exception of one, all were gentle in spite of their stubborn streaks. The first one in my memory was a huge Jersey, truly outsized for her breed. Her name was Daisy, far too innocent a name for the only ugly tempered cow I have ever met. She respected my father deeply, but believed I was a kind of small debris to be disposed of. She devoted her years on the farm to that theory.

Her first attempt at eradicating me was when I was not quite three years old. She had found her way through the pasture fence, one of her delights in life. Spying me at play on the lawn, she rushed up to me with head lowered, scooped me up with her fine set of horns and tossed me into the air as if I was a rag doll. Except for having the wind knocked out of me, I was unhurt.

My father arrived just in time to intercept her second attempt.

Daisy and I shared a mutual agreement from then on. She hated me with a purple passion and I feared her. I made it a point to always know what side of the fence she was on.

As I grew older I would be sent to the gardens either to pick something or take a message to my Dad if he was there. The vegetable gardens were independently fenced in on the inside of the fenced pasture, and their succulent contents were a constant source of temptation to the cows. On these errands I had the fastest route to safety all mapped out. Daisy seldom failed to sense my presence, and I couldn't count the times I barely leaped over, or rolled under, a fence with her lowered head and snorting breath at my heels.

My Dad tried to cure my cowardice by telling me that Daisy chased me because I ran from her, and that if I would only have the courage to stand my ground and face her down she would respect me and leave me alone. I tried this theory just once, but I proved no match for Daisy's wall-eyed glare and thundering approach. Once again I cleared the fence with seconds to spare.

Daisy was an incredible producer of fine calves and vast quantities of rich milk. But even though Dad was a good feeder and kept his cows fat and shining clean, Daisy had an insatiable lust for food, especially if it beckoned from the wrong side of the fence. She was a leader, an instigator, and could breach any barrier.

Cow care includes two milkings seven days a week, but at times my folks would plan a day away. It was inevitable that when we returned in time for the evening milking, the cows were either not home at all or had committed some bizarre act.

Daisy loved getting into the small orchard whenever she saw apples on the ground. Of course, the gang followed her. On one of our returns from a day's outing, the cows had all been eating quantities of green apples that had fallen during a rainstorm. As we drove up the hill to the house and saw the cows stumbling around, my mother said, "Oh, John! The cows are drunk!"

The apples had fermented and, because of their complicated digestive system, the cows were indeed blatantly drunk. When Dad encouraged them to head for the barn they literally staggered up the lane, front legs crossing and uncrossing, their eyes rolled around like marbles in a bottle. It was wildly comical. However, they were also bloated and needed help. Mother and I helped Dad walk and medicate the cows all night. They were quite mollified the next day, probably hungover.

The next time the cows attacked the orchard in our absence was another scene to remember. If only there had been video cameras then! Dad had left a long wooden ladder against an apple tree as he had been picking apples. A few remained on the ground. There was a world of space on each side of the ladder for Daisy to get at the apples, but she figured the best way was to insert her horned head between the ladder rungs. How she did it is a mystery.

When we arrived home, Daisy was moping around with the ladder extended almost equally from each side of her neck. When Dad approached her, she bumped the ladder on a rock and then was off careening around the pasture. Both ends of the ladder were hitting the ground as she galloped along, causing her more panic. Dad was in hot pursuit, cavorting, skipping, leaping to miss the ladder. When he did catch Daisy, he had to use a saw to remove the ladder from her neck.

Daisy delivered the final straw unto her own back by getting into Dad's garden just once too often. Her bovine guile had led her through every fence he could devise—wood, barbed wire, page, and finally electric. All the cows had had a moist sniff of the new electric wire and that was enough. Not for Daisy.

After laying her wet nose against it a few times, she found she could kneel down, slide her head sideways under the wire, and trim back the bordering vegetables quite nicely with her long neck and tongue.

Dad met the challenge by rigging a metal aerial on her bell collar. She looked like an interplanetary experiment. When she next kneeled at the fence, the aerial connected and in her surprise at the unexpected jolt, she reared up and with her huge bulk tore out a great section of the single strand fence, freeing it from the battery source.

Daisy soon realized that the entire garden was now hers to devour. The rest of the troops joined in when they saw the goodies their leader had just laid open for them. All were feasting royally with Daisy trailing festoons of wire from her aerial. What they had not eaten they trampled. Among the tender favorites they all had a goodly helping of green onion tops. These carried their flavor through to the milk, which had to be discarded for several days.

Daisy was given to a good home without children or gardens. I must confess to a wonderful sense of freedom when I saw her stepping in the cattle trailer!

SING A SONG, CATCH A COW

My efforts to follow my father's advice and stand my ground when Daisy the cow was about to chase me were to no avail. Respect for my courage was not in Daisy's character. Each time I saw her lower her head and begin snorting, I was on my way to sail over the fence with her hot breath at my heels. For nine years I continued to embrace cowardice until Daisy moved on.

I loved the other cows, and my subsequent cow memories are happy—drinking a dipperful from the milk pail, warm, frothy and Jersey-yellow rich, leading the cows one at a time to the stone-lined well and hand pumping big wooden tubs full of water.

The cows seemed to love the trip from the barn to the well, walking with dignity and carrying their tails in a delicately curved S. It was worth pumping water to watch them drink. Above their gray rubbery noses was a white satin band that wrinkled endearingly with each slurping intake of water. When they lifted their heads for breath, silvery streamlets dripped from their velvet, whiskered chops. Their soft eyes gazed around, and I waited for what I loved to see—their beautiful plush-covered, deeply cleft chins.

High on my list of cow enjoyment is cow breath. It is a warm essence of the tender grasses of a sun-drenched field, sweet and clover-clean.

Newborn calves are right up there on the list too. Our calves were silken-soft, playful, and held their necks up to be scratched. They nursed their mothers with deep contentment, cleft chins held high, dark eyelashes lying on their cheeks, and foamy milk cascading down the sides of their faces.

When a calf was a few weeks old, Dad would let me put a cupful of dark garden earth through a fine sieve and feed it to the calf, who greedily lapped it from my hands. This natural bacteria started its rumen working and the calf craved it.

In my twelfth summer, Dad injured his hand severely when sharpening a scythe. Sulfa drugs were new and prescribed to prevent infection, but an allergic reaction confined him to bed in a dire state for six weeks. His own remedy of a plantain leaf spread with balsam pitch would have been better.

Dad's illness left my mother and me with the total cow care. She was cooking three meals a day on a wood stove for our fourteen summer inn guests. All this was without benefit of electricity which did not come to Shore Road until four years later.

Mother and I milked the cows together and the rest of their care was mine. I loved it. I cleaned out the manure gutters each morning, washed and brushed the cows before they were milked, and turned them out to pasture. Getting them back to the barn for evening milking was a challenge to my wits and patience.

After the hay had been harvested from the big field, the cows were free to graze on it. It was a long distance through a wooded lane. By five in the evening the cows were usually at the pasture gate near the house lowing softly to come home to the barn to be milked. If they were not there, they would soon respond to Dad's reaching call of "Come boss, come boss." But not so for my puny efforts.

I knew if I caught one cow the rest would follow, so with looped lead rope in hand, I would walk the forested lane to the field. There was deep pleasure in going there because the field was bounded by Greenland Cove on two sides and looked out to Ram Island, the dark spruce of Hog Island, and on out to sea.

There are several fine homes in that field now, but in my youth it was wild and free, and I knew where the fringed blue gentians grew. Many the horse-drawn hayrick have I ridden on after helping to pitch it full of new mown hay.

My forays to the field in search of the cows resulted in them letting me get just so close before they skittered away, tails a-twirl and hind legs merrily fanning the air. They respected and loved my father, and never would have tried this with him, but I was small and fun for them to tease. Just cow humor apparently.

My only option was to select the oldest cow and run her down. This was hard on both of us. Soon I learned they didn't take off quite so quickly if they didn't see the rope in my hand. Keeping it hidden behind my back gave me a better chance to throw it over the horns of the nearest one if I was quick enough. None of the cows were polled, all had horns, and I was quick only half the time.

Now that I have long since ceased caring if people laugh at me, I can reveal my secret cow-catching method. I discovered it by chance. I must have been especially happy one late afternoon in the field because I was singing while approaching the cows with the rope behind my back. There was no one to hear and I was putting my heart and lungs into it.

To my amazement the cows stood stock still and gaped at me. I believe they would have raised their eyebrows if they had any. Continuing to sing, I walked right up to the nearest one, usually a renegade, and caught her with the first cast of the lead rope.

I'll never know if the cows were amused or horrified, all I cared was that singing worked. Every time. Burl Ive's versions of "On Top of Old Smoky" and "Down In The Valley" were my best numbers. Mother and I both admired Jeanette MacDonald's singing and sometimes I threw in "Ah, Sweet Mystery Of Life." This song had several very high notes that I could only reach by screeching. The cows were even more awestruck by this one. No wonder. I am still thankful there was nobody to hear me.

.Much as I loved the comforting smell of a sheep barn in later life, I will always have a warm spot for the rich and earthy aroma of a cow barn, so redolent of contented, peaceful animals. These are not scents generally appreciated. They have to be part of one's life to be understood. They represent a sense of belonging perhaps, a feeling of home—that we share a solid, secure place with our animals, that we are all living beings depending on each other.

I am reminded of a young boy, probably ten or twelve years old, who I met one summer at the shore in Round Pond. It was a hot day and he was diligently struggling empty lobster bait barrels up the float ramp to place on the dock. His rubber boots were covered with fish scales, and the bait barrels were pungent in the sun. I remarked to him that he was doing a good job.

He replied, "Thanks, but I guess I stink. Some people don't like that smell." I told him not to worry, we had a farm and raised sheep.

The boy said, "Gee, I bet they stink too!" I replied, "Well, some people may think they do, but it is a good honest stink just like your bait barrels. Be proud of your work, and don't care what anybody thinks!" His smile was broad and beautiful.

"SEE MOM, I TOOK MY SHOES OFF!"

Since technology has provided us with video cameras some comical experiences have been recorded. One we remember vividly took place a few years ago.

A couple of friends we met at a campground shared a video that their daughter made for them with us. Fred and Lucy had sold their home in Virginia to move to central Florida within a few miles of their daughter, Myrna, who had a small farm where she raised a variety of animals.

The new home was in a sanctified gated community. Fred and Lucy both revered shine, polish, and the purity of white. This was reflected in their comfortable but pristine home with white carpeted floors throughout and rooms that appeared constantly ready for a photographer from *House Beautiful Magazine*.

After they had moved and settled, Fred and Lucy came to Maine to spend a week with us. Myrna volunteered to look after her parents' new home while they visited us. Myrna knew her folks would be eager to describe their house to us, and she decided to make a video of it room by room to send to Maine. When it arrived with Myrna's accompanying message, Fred popped it into our TV and we all saw a lady friend of Myrna's operating the camera while Myrna conducted the tour. As she entered the white tile foyer of the house, Myrna carefully removed her shoes, explaining herself as she went:

"Mom and Dad don't want me to bring any residue from my farm into their house. See, Mom, I took my shoes off and I didn't bring the dog because I know you don't like the fact that he slobbers on things. So please be at ease because he isn't with me."

Myrna continued to speak as the camera panned the lovely foyer and graciously elegant formal living and dining rooms. She then moved into the glittering kitchen and the impression of perfection was immediate.

Incredibly, for a few seconds, a large Nubian goat splotched with black, white, and brown and sporting long floppy ears was seen following Myrna, its hooves clattering on the white tile of the kitchen floor. No one says anything about it, and then it is gone as Myrna continues around the kitchen talking of the sparkling appliances on its center island.

Moving to the refrigerator, she said, "Mom's refrigerator is always perfect, never any stale food. Even when she isn't here the food is always extra fresh!" As proof, Myrna opened the door and we saw a large, colorful rooster squatting on the refrigerator' s bottom shelf. His red comb and wattles fluttered as he clucked inquiringly at the light coming on suddenly. Myrna made no comment as she closed the refrigerator door.

Further into the house she reviewed her mother's lacy, ruffled, rose-budded bedroom.. Next was the attached bathroom gleaming with crystal, marble, and elaborately embroidered towels. Myrna slid the etched glass shower door open. A fat brown-and-white pot-bellied pig was sitting on his hind end in the tub. He had a large pink bow around his neck that matched his undulating snout. He grunted as his small, piggy eyes regarded Myrna questioningly. Without a word or a glance at the pig, Myrna closed the shower door.

She announced, "Dad's Room." It was neat and masculine, but with a snow-white carpet. A very large, shaggy pony was standing on the carpet swishing his tail and *whuffling* his nose over the white bedspread. He was ignored. Myrna finished the tour for a few more minutes as the flop-eared goat followed her around bleating in the hysterical fashion of Nubian goats.

Myrna made no comment on the animals, seemed not to see them, and ended by saying, "I hope you enjoyed visiting Mom and Dad's new house. As you can see, and probably know, they pride themselves on keeping a super clean and neat home." Then she took her shoes from the foyer and went outside to put them on again. Lucy and Fred were gape-jawed, and we were choking with laughter. Knowing their daughter's sense of humor, they couldn't help joining us.

The video was flawlessly executed, and later Myrna described what she had gone through to create it. She had piled the appearing animals into her stock trailer and had some heavy explaining to do getting it through the community gate. Although the video was smooth and seemed uninterrupted, it actually had been delayed many times as Myrna rushed her animals between house and stock trailer for the takes. She managed to accomplish the filming of each one before the animals had a chance to commit any sins in the house. She had carefully cleaned their feet before letting them enter. She also cleaned the house thoroughly after the photography.

It was an arduous production but well worth it. Myrna said that several times she and her friend with the camera literally had to lay down to laugh at the antics involved. When Lucy and Fred returned home, they were happy to report that their house was completely spotless.

Don't Tell Me You Are
Going to do This Again!

Many years ago we wanted a week's getaway, so we rented a bungalow on the Abaco Islands in the Bahamas. We had never been there, but we'd heard that our favorite activities of swimming and snorkeling were excellent there. The only way to reach the island was by a small plane out of Fort Lauderdale, Florida. The little island airline consisted of any contraption that could get off the ground. Our craft was like a box trailer with wings. It flew with the same grace. After roaring and pounding around in the air, we landed safely at the island's tiny airport.

The simple bungalow was old and being rented until it was sold. The island's electricity came on and off at will, for hours at a time either way. Water was scarce but not a problem, as the shower faucet fell off the wall the first time we used it. The place was airy with a pleasant outdoor patio. The food closet's yield was a half bag of dry cat food. We had expected to shop for groceries in the one existing store, so we went into the small town with list and the provided golf cart. Bicycles were the regular means of travel and cars were few due to gasoline price and limited availability.

The grocery store was memorable. The supply boat came once a week and it was due in two days. It was apparent that anything worth consuming had been bought up the day the boat was unloaded. The produce shelves were empty except for an open container of a gelatinous green mass that overflowed its shelf. The sign said it had once been alfalfa sprouts. The open meat case offered only scrawny chickens wearing most of their feathers. They looked like the remains of a voodoo ceremony. We settled for canned items—ham, veggies, and fruit.

Thinking there would be fresh seafood available, we asked a lady customer if she knew where we might find some rock lobster. She gave us a wooden stare and said coldly, "Don't know. I never eat anything that had a face or a mother."

We were here for sun and swimming and both were in abundance. The endless beach was glorious, with white sands and crystal water patterned in lovely lavender reflections as well as very few people. We swam and snorkeled most of the daylight hours and went to bed early. When thinking of this island, I remember the cats. They were everywhere, belonging to nobody. They just kept multiplying. The local veterinarian kindly gave an occasional day when people caught what cats they could and he neutered them. He couldn't keep ahead of the production.

During our first evening at the island bungalow, two thin cats appeared—a black and white accompanied by a blurred calico. They were friendly and hungry, so we put out the cat food from the closet. Next day we brought in a week's supply of goodies for them. The two faithfully came to be fed every morning, and each night they would slip through the partly open door. They cuddled into each of our necks, purring and snuffling in our ears as we all fell asleep together. We badly wanted to take them home with us, but the complications were prohibitive.

We had flight reservations for the day we were to leave. The previous day, a wild storm had raged and there had been no flights, so everyone that planned to leave the island on the stormy day now had to fly the day we were leaving. Everything the airline had that looked like a plane (and even crafts that didn't) was in service the day we left.

Our baggage was taken away and we watched the planes being loaded. The nearest to us was a small craft with a long, pointed fuselage. Baggage was being loaded into the pointy end. Jim and I remarked to each other about what a terrible time the men doing the loading were having trying to stuff it all in. Looking closer, we noted that some of it was our baggage they were attempting to cram when they had to take out a big amount of this cargo and re-pack the whole collection. There was no doubt it was destined to be our plane.

When it was boarding time, we approached the craft with trepidation that grew by the moment. Great gobs of thick black grease streaked back from the fuselage. There were many dents and dings plus missing rivets. Inside were six single seats on each side. They were ripped and ragged, pieces of chrome hung loose. The whole plane looked like it had been retrieved from a junk yard. We sat across from each other. The pilot and co-pilot explained how, if needed, we would find flotation devices beneath the seats. Looking there, it seemed that a crowbar would be necessary for removal. I whispered to Jim that I didn't think we would need to worry—with all the baggage in the front end she would never take off anyway, and they would have to give us another plane.

We buckled the worn seat belts and the ride began. The runway was short, so power had to be poured on quickly. The plane's laboring lift was so long and hard we barely cleared the tree line. The craft wallowed awhile, then settled into a reasonable progress for about twenty minutes before building clouds appeared and the ride became very rough. As the wings went up and down, the plane seemed to move ahead one side at a time. Every part of it shook and shuddered. We came into a massive black cloud bank and suddenly the craft plunged down fifty stories with the speed of an express elevator. My heart didn't catch up. The tall men, including Jim, smacked their heads on the ceiling. A passenger seat was directly behind the pilot (there was no private cockpit), and the man sitting in it wrapped his arms around the back of the pilot's seat and kept them there.

We rose back up the fifty stories, then dropped again. The pilot and co-pilot conversed through radio telephones. We couldn't hear anything because of the deafening engine. Jim told me he could see the compass and that we had changed course. We learned later that was because we were on the edge of a severe thunderstorm. I thought we were actually in it. Every moment we were still in the air seemed like a gift. Suddenly, it sounded like the plane was being bombarded by hundreds of soda cans. I remember thinking, "There! She's coming apart. I knew she would. Nothing could look and act like this and stay in one piece in this weather." Jim shouted to me, "It's only a hail storm, it'll pass."

Somehow, it eventually did. The sun came out and we landed in Fort Lauderdale. The pilot jumped out and helped the passengers onto the tarmac. When it was my turn I said to him, "I have just one thing to say to you!" He looked at me like he was expecting a complaint. I continued, "My God, you are good!"

He smiled. I asked, "Don't tell me you are going to turn this thing around and go back to the island in that weather for another load?"

He assured me he was going to do just that. I replied, "You are one courageous man!"

He laughed and said, "That's what my mother tells me, but she won't ride with me!"

Whatever his plane looked like, he knew its stamina and what it could take for abuse. Still, I understood his mother's decision.

How to get a Seat on a
Crowded Subway

There was a news story recently about a beautiful pet tiger that somehow left its owner's control and had to be destroyed. Without hearing complete details, it would be difficult to say if the destruction was necessary. Charming and friendly as they can be when humans bring them up from birth, all wild animals are born with the feral instincts to fight for survival in their natural habitat. Whether or not they should become pets is an open question.

Loving cats as we do, we can understand that having a pet lion or tiger would mean having a lot more cat in one package. We have always been captivated by the magnificence of large felines, their fierce grace and elegance of form, but we are happy to live with the smaller versions.

Many years ago I had a personal experience with a huge tiger. *Very* personal. It was the winter of 1950, and Jim and I had to pack ourselves off to New York City in an effort to do some concentrated earning to replace our old lobster boat with a new one. We also needed a down payment on the purchase of our farm.

Jim worked fourteen to sixteen hours a day starting at night driving a fuel truck for American Airlines at La Guardia Airport. I worked days as a secretary. We saw little of each other for the five months of our city exile, but our goals were worth it. We did finally manage to have an afternoon off together and felt we had to find a place where there were at least a few trees and some animals. The Bronx Zoo was the best option.

While it was enjoyable to see the variety of animals, it was also sad to observe the prison life they endured. Now, confinement in zoos is naturalized as much as possible, but back then animals were mostly forced to live in squalid cages.

Our last visit of the afternoon was with the lions and tigers. Lions who should have been sleeping in the shade of a tree or stalking their native plains, were lying despondently in the corner of a small cement floored cell, their eyes devoid of inner spirit.

The tigers were at the far end of the aisle of lions. There was no glass in the cage fronts, only iron bars. A gutter in front of the cages carried off the flushing of the pens, and an iron rail in front of the gutter kept observers back. At the last cage on the end of the row, a tiger had been roaring with deafening intensity and continued, barely pausing to draw breath. Just one person, a woman, was standing in front of the cage. I couldn't tell if she was teasing the tiger, but while Jim was looking at the lions I went to investigate.

The tiger, a male, was pacing the short length of his enclosure. His great padded feet measured four or five steps before he returned to the opposite wall, all the while bellowing his anguish and frustration as he continued his monotonous ritual. The woman was quietly watching him and I stood beside her, my heart aching for the plight of this beautiful creature doomed to his dank jail.

In a move almost too quick to perceive, the tiger lifted his tail and whipped his hind end against the bars. I had seen enough tomcats spraying their territory to know what was coming next. But this took place in such a flashing second I only had time to turn sideways in my effort to leave, and no time to warn the woman beside me. She took a full frontal drenching from chin to ankles, and I was soaked shoulder, arm, to the hem of my long coat. Anyone who has had a tomcat knows how malodorous this spray can be. Multiplying the output of a tomcat to the tenth power in terms of odor and volume doesn't come close to that of a tiger.

Jim, who had not witnessed the tiger scene down the aisle, literally smelled my approach, and with twinkle-eyed humor heard my story. We had to take the subway back to where we lived. It was a bitterly cold winter day and I couldn't be without my coat. The time happened to be rush hour and the subway trains were packed. We were given so much space due to tiger stench that we actually found seats. We were also the objects of disgusted looks and muffled remarks. We had to chuckle together, knowing that explanation wasn't possible.

No cleaning establishment would have allowed me in the door with that coat. Fortunately it was an older hand-me-down, so it was left to the imagination of the sanitation department. I don't believe they guessed it was a tiger's justifiable comment on humanity.

FELINITY

Our five inch-thick second edition unabridged *New Twentieth Century Webster's Dictionary*, first copyright 1904, describes felinity as "the quality of being feline." The characteristics of felinity draw many of us into sublime devotion toward those who possess it: cats.

How to explain our servile fawning toward these charming beings, and why bother explaining? If it is necessary to explain, it won't be understood anyway. Those of us who must have at least one cat in residence fully understand our fatuous yearning to share life with these fascinating beasties.

Mr. Webster has also given me an appropriate picture of the word "fatuous." One of its primary meanings is "complacently stupid." The word "complacent" means smug and self-confident. There are so many ways to be stupid. I have probably indulged in most of them, but I have become fond of the word "fatuous" and the fact that I can be complacent and smug about my stupidity.

Cat lovers know how haughtily independent and self-centered cats can be, but we also know their capability of giving boundless affection and comfort. Jim and I have always had a passion for them, and many cats have brought us joy through our sixty-eight years of marriage. There are too many to describe beyond these few—a pair of Siamese given to us as rescues. Each night this pair, Cleo and Si-Ling-Shi, would settle on our pillows in a semicircle around our heads, purring a soft song that lulled us into slumber.

It has been said that Siamese cats are noisy and cantankerous. Not so with these two. Their meows were distinctive, but seldom used. They didn't bite or scratch. In our opinion, a life shared with cats is not complete without at least a Siamese or two. Their coffee, ebony, and sapphire-eyed beauty, their grace and loving charm are incomparable.

Sandy, on the other hand, was a big clumsy lump of a cat, a graceless but lovable slob. Short-haired, emerald-eyed, sand and black-striped, he was sweet and complacently stupid. He chose places to nap that could—and did—result in his falling to the floor.

Sandy loved paper bags, and if one was hastily left on a tabletop or chair he would crawl inside to nap, first rolling around in an effort to settle until he rolled over an edge and onto the floor with a mighty thunk. Whenever there was the sound of a heavy object falling, we knew Sandy had been sleeping in a high place.

A lobsterman we knew had a twenty-pound marmalade cat named Twister. Each evening, our friend shared a boiled lobster with him. After his succulent supper, Twister would choose a braided rug, stretch his tangerine-striped body on his back with both front paws behind his head, and purr himself to sleep. His sleeping position was so unique our friend was once offered twenty dollars for Twister—a tempting price back in those days—but no sale!

Each of the cats we belonged to had the special personalities that are part of felinity. All had names, but most responded to our fatuous calls of "Pussifer," "Pooty-Ooty," or some other complacently stupid term. I remember a gentlemen bringing a huge cat into a veterinarian clinic and shyly announcing its name as "Stew Pot." I imagine there was a mild sin committed by the cat involving a pot of stew.

Felinity rewards us with silken fur leanings, brittle whiskery, and sandpaper tongue affection, rich gifts for being fatuous.

Bringin' in the Hay

When haying season arrives, I think back to the days when my husband Jim and I were sheep farming. Harvesting hay is an activity critical to weather, and our attention was focused on forecasts and all the folklore we knew.

My diary notes remind me of a typical day of bringing in the hay. Fog and rain can be the biggest problems at haying time. We needed a three-day window of sunshine. When the weather man came through with his glorious forecast of at least three consecutive days of sun, out came the hay mower, rake, tedder, and baler. On this day it was all a snare and a delusion. In full faith of the forecast, Jim mowed the field on the first sunny day. The next day came in cloudy with rain predicted for the afternoon. So much for the three days of perfection.

When the hay was down, we were committed. So, as we had often done in the past, we scrambled together our usual hay-loading crew and Jim tedded, raked, and baled hay for the entire day (a tedding machine drawn by the tractor fluffs the hay and helps it to dry). There had been little dew the night before, and the crop was dry enough to save if we could get it into the barn before rain.

On every trip around the field we glanced often at the sky. Clouds darkened by the hour and the wind smelled of rain. Our process included Jim never getting off the tractor, me watching the windshield and side mirrors of the big and old logging truck I was driving, and the crew bending and lifting throwing bales that *thunked* onto the truck to be carefully arranged by the designated stacker. The diesel tractor hummed, the baler pounded the hay into the baling chamber, the knotters clanged as they tied and cut the twine. Sound and motion was smoothly executed, the symphony of the harvest.

There was no stopping in that long day, and we got every last wisp of hay off our field and stuffed into the barn just as the rain began. The satisfaction was like winning a contest. Mowing a big area of good hay and losing it to rain is a hard loss.

Hay is a unique product, a wild natural growth full of nutrients, especially if cut and dried quickly. Each of the variety of grasses provides qualities of its own—timothy, clovers, red-top and cow-vetch, its purple-blue blossoms, and that of the rose and white clovers perfectly preserved in sun-dried color. Cows and horses like the coarser stemmed grass while sheep nuzzle around in the hay racks for the finer fibers, particularly relishing the vetches.

A barn filled with fresh, sweet scented hay is to farm people as a bank full of gold would be to a miser. The crisp bales are eagerly awaited by the animals. Things that are hidden in the mowed windrows aren't sorted out by the baling machine as it picks up and packs the grasses tightly in the baling chamber. One winter morning I was reaching into the hay pile for a bale and thinking, "How nice! This one even has a handle!" It was a dried garter snake perfectly curved on top of the bale in a handle shape, its head and tail secured by the hay twine. Not my kind of handle.

As we traveled around the field with the tractor, truck, and mechanical equipment, I thought back to how my father harvested his hayfield bounded by saltwater. He used a huge scythe which constantly needed to be sharpened with a whetstone. Then we raked with big wooden-toothed rakes, followed by pitch forking the loose hay into a long hay rick. It was pulled by a team of draft horses, then off-loaded by pitch fork into the hay mow of the barn. It was heavy, hard, time-consuming work.

A hay field next to the ocean is the worst to deal with weather-wise because of its proximity to fog. Satellites, radar, and informed weather forecasters didn't exist when my father hayed. Those who farmed, fished, and spent the better part of their time outdoors developed a sense for the weather as well as some sayings to help their daily plans, such as:

"Clearing skies never come from the east."

"Blue sky in the north generally means clearing will occur that day."

"If there is a ring around the moon, however many stars are within the ring is the number of days before rain or a storm."

"When dew webs appear on the grass in the morning it will nearly always be a clear day."

"If the wind blows so the underside of tree leaves are showing plainly it will rain within twenty-four hours."

"A sun dog, a rainbow colored appearance a short distance from the sun, means a storm within a day or two. As does a mackerel sky."

For us, when the wind brings the ringing of the New Harbor bell buoy, we know a storm is coming soon. This omen rarely fails. Not all folklore is infallible, but it comes amazingly close to accuracy. We are now in an age when the grain and grocery stores will make up for a family farm's harvest loss. But way back then, we all survived only on what hard work and weather savvy could produce.

The sweet sweep of a newly mowed field soon produces an emerald velvet cover, and by September it will provide a second crop of tender, leafy hay. To the sheep, and cows this crop is dessert. The haying equipment will come out of the barn again, we'll listen to NOAA, scan the sky, keen the wind, and hope not to hear the New Harbor bell buoy toll out our rain signal.

GREEN SWAMP AND RUNAWAY SHOW SHEEP

For many years, Lewiston, Maine had a very fine trotting horse race track, and it was next to this that the annual fair was held. During our first years of showing our sheep there, the beautiful old grandstand was still being used. It was a massive structure, old, narrow, and towering in height.

From beneath its scrolled and scalloped eaves tremendous letters proclaimed "GRAND STAND." Flags flew gaily from the ridgepole and great red, white, and blue banners were gathered in their centers and draped across the front of the grandstand. It seemed to have been suddenly transported from a Currier and Ives print, and I used to feel that the ladies walking past it should have parasols, wear hoop skirts and bonnets, and the gentlemen long tailed coats and tall hats. Because of structural decay that was beyond repair, the grandstand was torn down. The bewitching atmosphere of stepping into the past when viewing this edifice disappeared with it.

Exhibiting livestock at the Lewiston Fair was very different from the others we attended since it was so close to the city. Railroad tracks bordered the back of the sheep pens, separated only by a tall board fence. The first year we weren't aware of the railroad behind the fence and when the midnight freight train came roaring through, we awoke inside the shuddering trailer convinced that the polar ice-cap had slipped and the end was upon us. The sheep wore their ears in an extended position for some time afterward, probably wondering what else was coming, but they did not panic.

Even though the city and the railroad track bordered two sides of the livestock area, we could still look in another direction to stretching pine forests and flowing fields of corn. It is one of my secret delights that from many places in most of Maine's larger cities one can look beyond to the wooded hills, gliding rivers, or the sea—a comforting reassurance that the city is limited and nature's healing presence endures close by.

The race track was not designed to be a fairground, and the sheep pens were snuggled between the racing horse stables with the railroad tracks in back of them. Our camper-trailer was backed up to a horse stable. A blacksmith shop was just beyond the galley window. Watching the farrier shoe horses while I prepared dinner was fascinating and often exciting, as not all horses were willing to submit to this necessity.

Trotters and pacers pulling their sulkies were in motion past the trailer windows at all hours, either going out for exercise or returning from racing, sudsy with lather from their efforts. After being unharnessed, they were walked quietly for a long while to cool down while covered in colorful checked blankets. Slender and spirited, they were built for speed. These horses were catered to in every way. Mingling with other pungent horsey odors from the rear of the stables was the lingering aroma of horse liniment.

The only electrical outlets available for our camping trailer were inside the stable in a horse stall. With the horse owner's permission, our cord was plugged into the nearest one. We often fell victim to a playful or bored horse who thought it a fine joke to yank the plug out with his teeth just when the coffee was perking or the toaster was half ready to deliver. Not a customary household hazard.

The racehorse owners were busy people. When not training or exercising their animals, they were grooming, placing their horse's feet in portable whirling baths, and mending harness and sulkies. They had old wringer type washing machines spotted around the stables for washing horse blankets. Even though the stables were old, the living area for the horses and tack was always neat and attractive. Every horse's wish was their owner's command.

People from all walks of life owned racing trotters and pacers. One retired farm couple in their late seventies raced at Lewiston for years. Their mare was their pride and delight, and the warm bond that flowed among the three of them was quietly evident. They came from a coastal farm and said they trained their mare all winter, taking her along the dirt roads of the blueberry barrens that skirt the sea. The horse was their year-round project and a source of purpose and joy.

One year at Lewiston Fair, the proximity of the railroad tracks added considerably to the excitement of sheep judging. Someone had brought a small flock of very heavily wooled sheep that were not accustomed to human beings in general and fairgrounds in particular. During the show, they frequently bowled their owners over into the sawdust of the show ring in their attempts to escape. One determined ewe slithered from the grasp of her handler and headed for the one opening in the board fence that was her size. This brought her right onto the railroad tracks. Choosing the direction that promised open country, she flung her head up and trotted along the tracks, picking her way nicely among the cross ties.

We took up cautious pursuit as a group, realizing from experience that getting quietly ahead of the sheep was the only way to turn her back. The territory on either side of the tracks was steep and did not lend itself to this maneuver. A long-legged lad with more stamina than strategy decided the only course open was to outrun the ewe. Those of us who have tried this before and gone down in exhausted defeat stood and watched the drama of futility.

When sheep and boy had been reduced to mere movement in the distance between the narrowing, shiny tracks, we followed along to see how things were progressing. The two had disappeared around a distant curve and, not knowing the train schedule, we hurried our pace in the event that modern locomotives may not be equipped with sheep and boy catchers. We found them nearly a mile from the fairgrounds.

The ewe, apparently impressed by the boy's speed, opted for cover instead of the straight-away. She ran down over the precipitous bank into what she may have thought was a large, green pasture. In fact it was a great stagnant pool in a big swamp, and was completely sur-faced with a four-inch cover of algae and slime. Sheep and boy were engaged in a mighty struggle in the center of this jungle scene. He was winning because even though he was submerged to his armpits in this loathsome slough, he could wade faster than she could swim. Her heavy wool was soaked, causing her body weight to increase sev-eral fold. Two of the ewe's owners waded in to help the pair get out.

Both sheep and lad were unhurt but nearly prostrate with weari-ness and had to be helped up the steep slope to the rail tracks which were the only way of returning. They looked like horrendous crea-tures of the swamp, something imagined by a science fiction writer. They were dripping, smeared, and festooned with thick strands and globs of bright green slime. It had penetrated, stained, and hung itself on every exposed surface. Fringes of it swung from the boy's elbows and the sheep's ears.

During the interminable distance back to the fairgrounds, we all had to take turns by pairs carrying the ewe. She was too tired and her fleece too waterlogged for her to walk. Inevitably each of us became liberally coated in the huge amounts of emerald sludge that came from the ewe's saturated wool. We stumbled along with her, laughing at each other's grotesque appearance, and ceased worrying about a pos-sible approaching train. We were sure the engineer would come to a shattering halt before he would risk forfeiting the chance to interview the first visitors from outer space.

As with all shows, this one went on when we staggered into the show ring after penning the runaway. I have always wished I could have been outside the ring instead of in it helping with sheep showing so I could have heard the versions spectators devised as to what could have happened to all the horrible-looking green people.

The noise of the adjacent race track was pleasant, but sleep was not possible until the races ended near midnight, so we took evening walks around the small fairgrounds. One night, we were standing at the racetrack fence near the finish line. It was the last race of the night. The winner and all the trotters had passed the finish line with the exception of one whose horse had broken stride and was laboring along many lengths behind. The fellow standing next to us had apparently placed his money on this lagging entry because as the horse and sulky finally crossed the line, he clutched the fence and in a tone trembling with frustration shouted at the driver, "You couldn't drive a piss-pot!"

All the animals were asleep, the fair visitors were gone, and as we headed back to our trailer the only moving creatures were two small ponies and their owner walking a distance ahead of us. Probably they had been giving pony rides for children through the day, and we figured they were going to the stables. We stopped for a moment to look up at a melon slice of new moon and when we looked ahead again, the man and the ponies had suddenly vanished.

The only object in sight was the old car that had been parked in their pathway. We were puzzled until we passed the car and saw the man getting ready to drive away. The back seat of the car had been removed and the two ponies were settled into the space. We regretted missing the spectacle of the loading.

The next day we would be loading our sheep and driving to the Oxford Hills and Oxford Fair, which we always referred to as Norway Fair because the fairgrounds were so close to that lovely town.

WE DON'T KNOW NOTHIN'

No matter how strong the fencing is on a farm, there are always a few animals yearning for what gourmet offerings may lurk on the other side of the fence. The anxiety of noting that cows or sheep are missing from the pastures is not just the tiring chase ahead, but the worry of what mischief they got into?

A lady we knew who had a dairy farm bordering a four-lane highway in midcoast Maine had a typical experience. Her husband was away on business and she was alone. In the early afternoon a Maine State Trooper came by to ask if she owned dairy cows, and if so, they were all over the highway a couple of miles north of the farm. The trooper had looked along the road for the first farm they may have come from.

The cattle had found a tender place in the fence bordering the road and, once the leader went through it, most of the remaining herd followed and headed up the highway, causing traffic problems, but fortunately no accidents.

The lady gathered a bunch of halters and some grain buckets, threw them in the pick-up truck, and followed the trooper. Several other troopers had blocked traffic at a point that was luckily near a rest area. This breed of dairy cattle, Brown Swiss, was particularly huge and, while gentle, their size was intimidating. The lady was a tiny woman, but the cows knew her and as they came to the grain she had strewed around the rest area, she haltered them one at a time and tied them to picnic tables. When the tables were full of tethered cows, she tied the rest to trees.

When her husband returned, they made several trips with their stock trailer back to the farm. The delayed travelers were entertained by a cattle roundup. Apologies and pursuing loose animals is part of farming.

There was an elderly lady living on a small island a short distance off the Downeast coast of Maine. She had a tiny farm that provided much of her food supply, with vegetables, a cow, hens, and a pig. She became very ill and knew she would not live through the winter. She asked two of her lobstermen friends, Tom and Joe, to dispose of her animals for her as soon as possible.

The two men succeeded in finding homes for the cow and chickens and their new owners transported them from the island. The pig was fated for processing, and Tom and Joe dreaded the challenge of loading the huge pig onto the barge. Beyond that was getting him into their pickup truck. To their surprise, the pig was most cooperative and seemed to enjoy his voyage on the water. When they reached land, he stepped up the ramp to the truck and settled his big hind end in a corner of the truck bed. As they drove along, the pig snuffled the passing air and seemed to be having a fine time.

The trip was to end in Bangor. When Tom and Joe approached the outskirts of the city, they began to encounter traffic lights. The pig did not like the stops or the traffic around him, and he began to pound around in the open truck bed. As soon the lights changed and they were on their way again, he sat down calmly. But at each light he became more excited. The traffic signals were increasing, and the pig was now leaping around wildly.

Tom was driving and Joe gave him a worried look and asked, "What are we goin't do if that big sum-va-bitch jumps outa this truck inta' all them cars?"

Tom was a quiet man of few words. His big hands tightened on the wheel and, looking ahead at the road, he replied sternly, "We don't know nothin' 'bout no goddam pig!"

Early 20th Century Childhood in Maine

My mother spent her early youth in Scotland, the land of her birth. Walking was mostly the mode of transportation in the Highlands. In fall or winter when the season was over for Mayfair House, Mother thought nothing of a fifteen mile walk. As a teenager I walked with her, and we shared our thoughts, her tales of Scotland, and the scenes around us.

When I was just beyond toddling, Mother went easy on walking distances. We only went the two mile round trip to the mailbox. Mother made snowsuits for me out of old coats and, while warm, they were exceedingly bulky. I can remember walking like a robot, arms stiff and extended, with knees that couldn't seem to bend. I believe I whined and grizzled a lot about it.

As a child, the worst part of my winter was having the common cold. It was the medicines for it that were obnoxious. I can still see and taste them in my memory. Two of the most foul commercial ones were Scott's Emulsion and Father John's Medicine. The first was thickly viscous white liquid that would hardly leave the spoon let alone go down my throat. Father John's was in a tall brown bottle with a picture of a long-bearded fellow who I pined to see being the victim of his own medicine. His brownish brew was another heavy liquid that looked disconcertingly like something I regularly saw in the cow barn. Though I never made the comparison, I doubt it tasted much better.

Reminiscing about these times with Jim, I learned he had endured some of the same dreadful cures, adding that his mother believed in a spring tonic of sulfur and treacle. The molasses would have been tolerable, but the sulfur was both revolting in smell and taste.

There were no vaccinations back then for childhood diseases and, like everyone, I had them all. Whooping cough seemed to go on for the entire winter. My parents tried everything to ease the cough, but nothing worked. Then an elderly neighbor offered a family recipe that should have been buried with his ancestors. He called it Rum-Dum. Although I had shuddered and gagged on those described above along with the horrors of castor oil, nothing could match Rum-Dum for the sheer abomination of its taste and quality.

I don't know all that was in it, but I remember flaxseed, a small amount of rum, and lots of licorice. There were probably other ingredients as well. This was also a thick brown concoction. My parents never forced these remedies on me, but they were very persuasive in a kindly way as to the good these odious doses would do me. To this day I cannot abide the taste of either licorice or rum.

Now our children have lovely fruit flavored pills and syrups, but best of all, preventive shots for most childhood diseases. Many home remedies are good, but proper nutrition tops the list.

I treasure one cure my father had for cuts and scrapes. With a pocket knife and small piece of waxed paper, drain a pitch blister from the trunk of a fir-balsam tree. Next, find a plantain leaf on lawn or garden edges. This flat-leaved weed is common. Apply pitch to the wound, cover with plantain leaf, then secure with adhesive tape. The wound will heal quickly, cleanly, and pain will be reduced.

One winter over fifty years ago, my mother was hospitalized with a severe case of pneumonia. Huge doses of penicillin saved her, but after returning home, she was unable to retain food. Dr. Powell reasoned that the penicillin had eliminated bacteria in her digestive system and suggested a good dose of garden dirt would be the cure.

He was right.

Since this illness occurred in mid-winter the ground was deeply frozen and snow-covered. But around a spruce tree on the lawn there was a small windblown bare spot, and my father chipped out some hunks of good black earth. After thawing them, he put them through a fine sieve several times. With a generous spoonful of the earth added to our rich Jersey cow's milk, Dad whipped up a pleasant drink for my mother. She was back to normal after a few days of this treatment.

Our finest medicines originated in the fields and forest in the first place.

EBENEZER AND THE STEEL CORSET

Aside from the very few Mayfair House visitors who had cars, my father met incoming guests at the Newcastle Railway Station. I loved going with him to see and hear that wonderful locomotive come roaring in, amidst its clouds of steam. Its wheels of steel grinding to a shuddering stop before the chuffing and huffing of released steam as passengers departed the coaches.

The late 1930s and '40s were what now would be considered laidback. This is an understatement. At the Mayfair House, the small group of guests lived close together in their daily activities. Amazingly, they got on very well and many formed lifelong friendships, even scheduling their vacations to be together again. Good moods were fostered by great food, scenic beauty, and relaxation.

Meals were served family style at the large dining room table and the rule was all-you can-eat. Mother didn't believe in serving what she called "filler foods." Hamburg or pasta in any form never appeared on the table. Each day of the week had set menus. Dinner could be creamy clam chowder (we dug the clams ourselves), steamed lobster and clams, roast ham, leg of lamb, prime rib, home-grown chicken, veal, or duck. All were accompanied by freshly baked bread and garden vegetables and fruit just picked from my father's massive gardens.

At breakfast, each of the fourteen guests could order what they wished. Nothing was written down, but my mother remembered all of it. With only a wood fire stove, she quickly produced boiled, scrambled, or fried eggs to order. Every egg was from our own hens, bacon and sausage from our pigs. Breakfast always began with long-cooked oatmeal just as my mother had cooked it in her native Scotland. Huge plates of newly churned butter and enormous pitchers of heavy cream from our cows were on the table at each meal.

Cholesterol and some other diet issues had clearly not yet been discovered. Nobody refused the rich and bountiful food or Mother's heavenly desserts of melting-crust pies, home-raised strawberries for shortcake, lemon pie with meringue mountains, cream puffs loaded with whipped cream and Mother's own magical chocolate sauce. The list of delights is long. There were often letters from guests about the ten or fifteen pounds they had gained in two weeks and how they were now dieting to be ready for next year's gourmet experiences at Mayfair House.

Some elderly couples came to the inn for the entire summer. One such pair was Mr. and Mrs. Ebenezer Stirling. I never heard Mrs. Stirling's first name. Not even Ebenezer dared to call her by it. He addressed her as "Missus."

Ebenezer was tall, thin, and white-mustached. He smoked a pipe and seldom uttered a word. This was understandable, since Mrs. Stirling ceased talking only to sleep. Maybe.

I recall Mrs. Stirling as a sort of quivering mass. Her abundant white hair was piled in loose heaps on top of her head and secured by tortoiseshell hairpins. Steel rimmed pince-nez were clipped to her nose. Her eyes were piercingly blue and went well with her stern and unsmiling visage. Three chins of graduating length and breadth descended from her face. She always seemed to be shaking her head in disapproval of something said and her hair, pince-nez, and chins shook in unison.

Mrs. Stirling's ample body was encased in corsetry. I suspected it was of cement construction until I saw her spare one when helping clean her room. It was an impressive structure of steel, canvas, eyelets, and yards of lacing. Poor Ebenezer had his morning and evening chores cut out for him. Mrs. Stirling could not possibly have gotten into or out of it alone. I marveled that she could move and breathe in it.

Her dresses were custom-made and all of pale blue plaid, but they couldn't conceal the fact that her corsets pushed her upper body into a strange overflow that fought for position with her multiple chins.

Mrs. Stirling held court every evening on the screened veranda or in front of the parlor fireplace if it was raining, unless she could be talked into a card game to stave off her ongoing speeches. Her monologues concerned her church bazaar activities and all the women who belonged to it. She described the ladies individually with three standard labels: worthless, lazy, or sinful.

Mrs. Stirling was a crushing bore, and those who hadn't learned how to escape were stultified into silent endurance. She repeated her repertoire every two weeks when a new group of guests arrived. However, she did have one story she related rather well, and it concerned her archenemy in the church group.

The tale was about a lady with whom she vied desperately for the reputation of who decorated the fanciest cakes for bake sales. Over the years, feelings and remarks finally erupted into action. According to Mrs. Stirling, at the preparation of one such sale, one hostile word too many was exchanged and they each picked up the other's cake and pitched them at each other.

Mrs. Stirling's cake scored, or I don't believe she would have told the story. The other lady's aim was poor and her cake went full bore into the church organ, splattering itself all over keys arid intricate carvings. Mrs. Stirling cackled with glee as she related the lady's ordeal of cleaning the organ and herself.

You're Going to Drown, Harry

Boating provides adventures of all kinds. I recall one related to us by Harry and Ellen, who had just bought a new twenty-five foot Bayliner live-aboard boat. They were making their first passage with it, planning to move out of Rockland destined for Portland. They were not yet fully familiar with operating the boat in anything more than calm seas. Brisk winds and a nasty chop soon came up, and their boat was dithering around like a cork. Harry didn't know about trim tabs and quartering seas because he was accustomed to river boating. Ellen was terrified and wanted out of this scene. Harry studied the chart and saw that the nearest sanctuary would be New Harbor.

They entered the harbor gratefully and dropped anchor in this calm refuge a short distance from Shaw's Wharf and restaurant. After resting and relaxing in their pleasant security, Harry felt he should clean the salt spray from the windshield and side windows. Grabbing some rags and window cleaner, he went at the job with the pride of a new boat owner. When the windshield was done, he began work on the side windows.

Although it was rough and the wind blew hard beyond the harbor, it was a warm and sunny day on the decks of Shaw's Wharf restaurant, which was packed with people enjoying fine seafood at the picnic tables. There is always something to watch in a harbor and many eyes were upon Harry and his vigorous efforts. I'll relate the rest in Harry's words.

"The salt wasn't coming off the side windows very well and, for some reason I'll never understand, I forgot I was on a boat and I stepped back for a better look. I stepped off the boat, straight down with a mighty splash. Ellen heard it and came running to the rail. She and I both know I can't swim, although I was seriously treading water. She can't swim either and began screaming hysterically: 'Harry! Harry! You're going to drown! Why did you do that? Why? What am I going to do? Oh, I hate this boat!'

"I was well aware of the show now going on for Shaw's avidly watching diners, and between clenched teeth I said, 'Shut up for Christ's sake and throw me that life ring!' She did, and I pulled myself along the boat and around to the stern where the swim ladder was. Amazingly, I still had the sopping wet polishing rag in my hand and, hoping I could make my audience think this was a planned event, I held the life ring with one hand and reached up to the stern to give it a few swipes with the rag as if this was the only way I could get at it."

The footnote to this story is that the next day was calm and Harry and Ellen reached Portland safely. They gained more experience that summer and became happy boaters. Harry didn't take swimming lessons, but now he waits to wash the windows with a hose while standing on the dock.

What You Don't Know
Won't Hurt You

It is my belief that anything that floats and can be called a boat is beautiful. They come in all sizes, varieties, and levels of expense. Because the Maine Coast is so famous for its astounding beauty and cruising range, we often see the super yachts of celebrities and people that aren't well known but who have a luxurious lifestyle very different from most of us. The old saying about seeing how the other half lives is interesting and amusing at times.

On a passage Down East one summer, Jim and I stayed in a marina in the Bar Harbor region for a couple of nights to wait out some weather. A number of other boats of all types were there for the same purpose. Our neighbor immediately across the dock was a large and impressive motor yacht. We were situated in such a way that the only view we had was of the huge boat and most of the activity taking place on her from stern to bow.

Early in the morning, the uniformed crew—fellows and girls—thoroughly wiped away the night's fog and dew from every deck, window, and protuberance on the vessel. Fluffy white lapdogs were taken up the dock for their morning walk. Dock lines were re-coiled, rails polished, and deck chairs wiped down. Inside there was dusting and the placement of fresh flowers.

In the afternoon when the yacht owners and guests had gone ashore, there was a big daily wash job complete with hoses, mops, and brushes. Not a grain of dirt nor a minute smear was allowed to besmirch this craft.

In the evening, crew uniforms were changed from dark to snowy white and there was constant fussing with cleaning of some sort. As we quietly enjoyed our simple evening meal inside our boat, we were a relatively short distance from the yacht owners dining in their salon, although of course we couldn't hear them. They were dressed in summer evening finery and the table was set with sparkling crystal, silver, white tablecloths, and flowers. All was elegance and grace.

Or so it seemed.

Because the yacht was berthed a full length across from us, we could also see food preparation in the galley even though it was a fair distance from the salon. The chef and his assistants were in spotless white uniforms and earnestly stirring, checking ovens, and flipping pans.

The assistants stirred soups and sauces by sticking their fingers (no gloves) into the mixes, tasting, and returning the fingers for a better assessment. When the main course was served in the salon, there were chops of some sort on the plates. One lady frowned and indicated that she was unhappy with her chop. The butler, or whatever his title was, bowed and took her plate away.

Back in the galley we saw the chop being removed by fingers from the plate and headed for a pan on the stove. Before it got there, it fell into the sink full of soapy dishwater. After some fishing around it was retrieved, rinsed under the faucet, and plopped into the pan. The lady seemed quite satisfied on its return.

What turned out to be a dessert sauce was being regularly tasted by an assistant using the same spoon throughout. It dropped to the galley floor at one point but was given a couple of shakes and back into the sauce.

When dessert was served, a complicated-looking mound of something copiously covered in sauce, one of the gentlemen tasted it before shoving it away and ringing the table bell for the butler.

The dessert was taken away. Back in the galley something that looked like it came from a liquor bottle was added to the pot of sauce. Apparently this improved the taste. After sucking on a few finger-fuls, the chef sat down with the pot and ate several big spoonfuls. He looked pleased but seemed to think there should be confirmation of his opinion from the assistants. All used the same spoon that was then used to ladle the improved sauce over the dessert.

There is a trite old saying that what you don't know won't hurt you. Maybe not.

Crow Charm

Crows have always had a place in my heart, even though I know their reputation is less than stellar in some circumstances. They are rugged, brassy-brave, noisy sometimes, but they appear to have a certain loyalty to their species. I love the beauty of a crow flying in the sunlight, its black satin feathers glinting with flashes of wine and blue. On the ground they hop in a clumsy fashion, but they can swoop and glide gracefully through a thick growth of trees in spite of their size.

Each morning, I put scraps and some bread at the edge of the woods for the resident crows. It provides a rewarding opportunity to learn some interesting things about them. In the fall, there was a small flock of five that came for breakfast. One crow would keep watch in a tall tree and then call excitedly when I approached with food. The calls varied in pitch and rhythm, long and hoarse or urgently staccato, sometimes just a gurgling sound. In the world of wild animals it is generally every creature for himself when it comes to food. This is not so with crows—the watch crow lets his friends know it's mealtime. I take this as an unselfish act. The lookout crow could easily remain silent, drop down to the food, and eat or take away all he wanted without passing the word. But he waits until the whole gang appears before approaching breakfast himself.

While washing morning dishes, I watch the crows as they pick up a slice of bread or a cooked egg yolk and fly away into the woods with it, returning shortly for more. I've wondered how they handle the food when they go into the woods. One winter day my curiosity was satisfied when one crow chose a tree at the edge of the woods near the kitchen.

He selected a thick branch and walked along it until he found some twigs growing upward from the branch that would firmly hold the food. Placing it in this kind of basket-like formation, he took several bites before walking back down the branch to a pocket in the tree that held some snow. Several beakfuls of it fulfilled his thirst before he went back to the remainder of the food.

Two of the five crows seemed to be a loving couple who separated themselves from the group. One bitterly cold winter morning after their breakfast feast, I saw the two in a big maple tree nearby. The sun had risen and was shining brightly on them as they sat on a thick branch. They were so tightly snuggled together there was no daylight between them. Their night-black feathers were fluffed out fully and they looked content soaking up the sun, occasionally turning heads toward each other so closely their beaks touched. All I could think of was a loving, married couple sunning together, and talking about the weather and what they should do for the day. Love can truly be anywhere.

Moose Escape Plan

Often I give thought to the happy fact that we don't have to travel hundreds of miles to see moose, whales, seals, or pine forests, or eat lobster that hasn't languished in a tank. We are right here where all these precious gifts live and belong.

My fascination with moose is lifelong and has ranged from apprehension in childhood to rapturous delight thereafter.

Among the many guests at my parents' summer inn, Mayfair House, there was a fellow who claimed to be a hunter and sportsman. Perhaps he was. Although he had not hunted in Maine, he kept the guests entertained with some intensely chilling stories, most of them about frightening scenes with moose.

One tale remains in my mind as the basis of my early apprehension towards moose. Actually, more like my outright fear. This hunter gentleman vividly described a long night in a short tree where he had taken refuge from an enraged bull moose. The moose belabored the tree with his huge rack of antlers through the night until he grew bored at dawn and wandered off, leaving the shaken hunter to climb down and hurry home. Each of the moose's assaults on the tree was related in graphic detail. Whether or not the story was true, it was memorable.

I walked a mile by myself through the woods on an unpopulated dirt road to meet the beech wagon that took me and others along the way to the one-room Muscongus School. Moose were in the area, but not as many as there are now. Although I hadn't seen one, I knew they were immense, and this hunter's story stayed with me through the ages of seven to nine. I was convinced that a moose was just waiting to chase me up a tree.

With this in mind, I made it a point to scope out trees at short intervals along the road. I selected those with substance and enough branches for quick climbing. I made trial runs on a regular basis. Playing in the woods and climbing trees was my kind of fun, so I had some good "moose safety stations" lined up.

The year I was in the sixth grade, Mr. Ifill picked me up in his beech wagon one morning and had just finished shifting gears when a massive bull moose crossed the road in front of us. This meant he was only a short distance from my road. Walking home that late afternoon was just a journey from tree to tree.

If we lived in a city one of my parents would have escorted me to school, but they knew I was in the safest of environments and probably felt that my fears needed to be replaced by courage and character. Never in those beautiful walks did I encounter anything that would harm me.

Now there is a primordial thrill at seeing these majestic royals of the forest. Standing at least six feet tall at the shoulders and weighing upward of one thousand pounds, their regal stance and noble heads make me catch my breath in awe. Moose were called "Moz" by the Algonkian Indians, which means "twig eater" in a loose translation (an apt description of their diet).

Our occasional trips to Rangeley Lakes and other northern areas provided many moose sightings. We were always watching the moose wallows, which are weedy, swampy spots where water plants grow for moose to eat. The roadsides in those regions look like passing cattle drives in spring because they are so trampled with moose tracks. Even with their great antler racks and big bodies, moose can vanish into dense forest as if by absorption.

A friend who lives in Aroostook County regularly drives an eighteen wheeler from there and often sees moose on the road in winter. He said that one night, he had to stop the truck and wait for twenty-seven moose to make their decisions about leaving the road. Winter traffic is scarce in Aroostook County. Some moose were lying down while others were walking around leisurely. Salt on the road's snow and ice was the big attraction—it was a tasty treat.

Moose are placid, peaceful animals and can be observed for a while if one is still and unobtrusive. There are times when common sense says retreat quietly and quickly if one encounters a bull moose during the rutting season, usually in September. They are unpredictable then, just as a cow moose with her calf should not be approached for photos or a closer look. Their front and hind feet are lethal weapons, and a lone moose has been known to fend off a pack of wolves with them. Enjoying a moose's presence is about respect. Each moose I see is a celebration of beauty to hold close to the heart.

BARNYARD SOCIETY
OF MALLARDS AND EMDENS

Domestic water birds on our North Country farm were a happy presence in the general society of the barnyard. Their comical characters, beauty, and daily actions were a source of laughter and delight.

One fall, our mallard duck family was sadly reduced by a concentrated fox attack that left only five drakes who spent a lonely winter as bachelors until early spring when we were given two mallard females. We thought they would be shy and timid in new surroundings. Not so. The five bachelors were sleeping peacefully in the barn, heads tucked into their wings, when the two females waddled directly up to them. Bumping their chests against the drakes, the females grasped them by their necks and shook them thoroughly. The clear message was "We are here now, and let there be no mistake about who is in charge!" The drakes were aghast at this strange assault, and they scuttled for the corral. Later, when ruffled feathers were restored, all seven ducks were peacefully floating in the pond creating a silver lattice-work on its surface as they paddled.

When spring approached, the barn came alive with the bleating of newborn lambs and the uproarious mating battles of the mallard drakes. With only two wives for five drakes, there were many days of combat. The problem was settled by one female having three husbands and the other having two in well-defined marriages. Even after this resolution, the drakes within each marriage spent more time fighting over the wife than paying attention to her.

The courting scenes among the mallards were entertaining. There were verbal messages on several sound levels and an intricate dance that required up-and-down movements of their necks. Nests were soon made and eggs deposited, unless there were mishaps in the corral before the nest could be reached.

The white Emden goose couple, not inclined to the clownishness of the ducks, sailed the pond like regal swans. Most of their morning was taken up with the serious business of the goose wife adding another large, chalk-white egg to their elaborate nest in the hay. The gander would stand over her while this was accomplished. These two were devoted mates and were seldom seen more than a few feet apart during the many years they were on the farm.

When it was time for the goose to sit on her eggs, the gander remained on guard beside her, his intelligent china-blue eyes aware of all that went on in the barnyard. He would reach under her occasionally to turn the eggs with his big yellow beak, then use the beak to gently smooth her feathers back into place. During the afternoons they covered the eggs with loose hay for warmth and disguise, had a quick meal, then took a hasty splash and drink in the pond before returning to the nest. If the goose was reluctant to leave the joy of a short swim, the gander firmly guided her back to the nest and their combined duty.

The two female mallard ducks (known as hens in the duck world) laid abundant eggs in and out of their nests. One day, we witnessed a comical scene while we were working in the barn. A hen duck couldn't get to her own nest on time and, since the geese were taking their pond break and she was passing their lovely big nest, she climbed in, laid her egg among the big goose eggs, and sat there awhile to rest. She was still on the nest when the geese returned from the pond.

There was no fussy ceremony of gestures or verbal scolding of the trespassing duck. The mother goose swiftly waddled up to her nest, clamped her big beak on the duck's neck, and swung her own long neck sideways to fling the duck off into the hay pile. The duck spiraled in a big arc before she landed headfirst, then gathered her wings and flew into the corral quacking in outrage.

We happened to be in the barn the day the big, pale-yellow goslings hatched. Among them was a single little golden duckling. The goose parents were loudly heralding the occasion as they poked at each hatchling. They listened to the whistling sound of their offspring, but they were obviously puzzled by the small quacking duck. Being the fine parents they were, they accepted it without further inquiry. Unlike duck families, both goose parents take equal responsibility in caring for their young. During a thunderstorm, we have seen the gander hurrying awkwardly to the barn with little fluffy goslings tumbling out from under his wings. He would quickly stop to scoop them up again. The year the geese raised the duckling as their own, we would see it in the pond swimming in single file with a goose parent at each end of the line. The geese were an exemplary couple and mated for life as many breeds of geese do. It was a beautiful relationship to observe.

This adoption reminded us of a year when a bantam hen had hatched a hastily dropped duck egg in her nest and she accepted it into her brood. As the duckling grew older, it was fun to see it rushing to the pond and enjoying a swim while the bantam hen stood at the edge frantically clucking at it to return from this forbidden element.

The ducks slept among the sheep or on top of their woolly backs in cold weather, sinking their orange feet into the warm fleeces. Nights when the pond was not frozen, the goose family knew that floating on the pond kept them safe from foxes. After twilight, they looked like white marble figurines on a black mirror.

Judgment Day for the Judge

The drive with each of our trucks hitched to stock or travel trailer through the twisting back roads from Norway to Union Fair was always a beautiful and challenging trip through more of Maine's forest, mountain, and lake country. We usually arrived at Union near sunset.

The Union Fairgrounds are cupped in a lovely valley among gentle hills bordered by a willow-hung river and nearby lakes. One year, we arrived a day before the fair initially opened, so the grounds were clean and freshly mowed. Even the carnival had not yet left Norway Fair and come onto these grounds. Only we livestock people were here settling our animals early so they would adjust to new pens and water supply.

The water at most fairgrounds was acceptable to the livestock unless there was noticeable chlorine in it. Our sheep were accustomed to the sweet, clear well water at home. If they did not seem happy with the new offerings, we sprinkled a little dry, flavored Jello over their water for a couple of days.

Over the years, camping areas at fairs were changed mainly for safety reasons, but in the early years the rule was settle where you could. In those times, we camped on a narrow grassy strip right next to the racetrack. It was closest to the sheep barns. From our trailer windows we could reach out, touch the fence rail, and feel the rush of wind from the trotters and pacers as they raced by and often kicked out clods of racetrack earth onto the trailer. It was exciting to be so close to this action, to hear the horses snorting, their powerful hoofbeats, see the drivers' colorful silks and hear their impassioned urging of the horses to gain more speed.

When sheep and trailers were in place, we would visit the general store to stock up for the week ahead. That fine emporium on Union Square carried everything from bandaids and bacon to deep well pumps. Worn-out sneakers or other clothing could be replaced at Susa-Belles.

During the first night, the carnival drifted in and began setting up. Looking at the complexity of the rides and accompanying machinery, it was hard to believe they could be so mobile, as most of them did not fold up conveniently. They were instead completely dismembered bolt, nut, and universal joint, then stacked in intricate formations so that reassembly won't require a blueprint.

The bone-weary, grease-begrimed crews worked all night. Incredibly, the empty field of the night before would become a flourishing midway by the next day with tightly placed game booths, towering rides, and food establishments sending forth essences of onion, green peppers, and burning charcoal. These aromas, combined with hot dogs, popcorn, newly trodden grass, and the wonderfully basic odor of barnyard animals, combine to create a fairground fragrance that, in our opinion, outstrips any other in reviving poignant memories. We always remarked that it takes about three days for a fair to start smelling really good.

Before the "open" or adult sheep show, the 4-H sheep members had their sheep show. One year their judge was unforgettable. He was a gentleman who had apparently come into a large fortune and felt it was time to make a radical change in his image from ordinary work-a-day person to a gentleman farmer. He had bought a large farm and stocked it with many sheep, some racehorses, and four stunningly massive Belgian draft horses. The Belgians were barely green-broke. Their new owner, Mr. Harrington, had been doing serious reading in the short time since he had acquired all these animals, and he believed his book learning made him ready to take on any task involving farm animal exhibitions.

Mr. Harrington had convinced the 4-H officials of his judging ability, and he appeared in the show ring certain he was dressed for the part—shining hightop boots, embroidery-encrusted western-cut shirt, and very tight jodhpurs that fit his rotund body like a second skin. The outfit was completed with a tall ten-gallon hat.

The 4-H boys and girls were neatly groomed, clean, and trim in their tan pants, white shirts, and green string ties. They viewed Mr. Harrington with their usual quiet respect and attention even though he had a markedly different way of examining their sheep for quality, breed-type, conformation, and trimming. He never seemed to have the proper name for the areas of the sheep he was describing in detail over the microphone. Nor was he able to make the watching public able to understand what kind of animal he was talking about. Undaunted, he kept up a running speech.

Mr. Harrington had us all mystified when he got down on his knees (unheard of in sheep judging) in front of a very large ram. He grasped it by the head, lifted its lips with his thumbs, then let them flap back into place after he had taken a good look into its mouth. He rose awkwardly, slapped the ram on its back, and declared it winner of its class because he "admired the membranes in its teeth." None of us ever forgot this bizarre wording. The 4-Hrs could not suppress a quiet snicker behind their hands. Harrington went on to explain his reason for placing the ram that was at the bottom of the class. He said, "This ram is in last place because I don't like the slop fat in his rib roots!" More hidden smiles.

Starting the next class, Mr. Harrington had to lean down quite far to make his examination of a very small lamb. The tightening distance of the lean put too much strain on the already stressed rear seam of his jodhpurs. They split from belt line to center crotch with an explosive rip, exposing his entire rear covered by red-striped boxer shorts. By now, neither 4-Hrs or spectators could hold back choking gurgles.

Harrington inquired if anyone had access to needle and thread. Nobody volunteered. Knowing I had a sewing kit in our nearby camper-trailer, my conscience was provoked into making the offer to stitch his jodhpurs so the show could continue for the 4-Hrs. He followed me to the trailer, and I told him he could remove the piece of clothing in the small bathroom and hand it to me around the door. He laughed and said that wouldn't be necessary as he dropped the pants where he stood. He was, of course, right in front of the screen door, with a clear view to the passing world of the public.

The couch was next to the door and he sat beside me clad only in his shirt, brilliant underwear, and huge hat. We were in full view of all, and he chatted companionably as if we were having afternoon tea. My needle flew and repaired the rip in record time. During the remainder of the sheep show, the children learned nothing they did not already know about sheep, but it was an experience they never forgot.

Early in the day, we would halter four sheep at a time and take them for a walk to exercise them. There once was a lovely trail through the woods at one side of the fairgrounds that was a favorite for walking the sheep. The trail ended in a small pasture with a hill and cemetery beyond. One day, we tethered the sheep in the pasture and took a quick walk to the cemetery. We were richly rewarded by finding the graves of Mima and Joel, the principal characters in Ben Ames Williams' *Come Spring*. This wondrous book is a poignant history of the settlement of Union. Having read it several times, we felt a kinship with Mima and Joel and wondered what they would think of this beautiful farming and blueberry country they had helped to pioneer if they could see it now.

On the last day of Union Fair, there is a colorful parade on the racetrack consisting of the Blueberry Queen, her fellow contestants, and a few antique cars. Local dealers enter their new offerings of farm equipment. There are floats representing clubs and services, but the greater part of the parade is made up of the livestock that fill the barns—beef and dairy cattle, draft horses, oxen, sheep, and goats. These are led by the exhibitors, but mostly by the young 4-Hrs in the families.

All of these groups pass the grandstand full of spectators as they continue around the racetrack and return to the barns. My husband Jim announced the parade for many years since we knew all the exhibitors as well as their breeds of animals and farm names. Mr. Harrington was on the scene as well. He was about to realize his dream of driving a four-horse hitch with his barely trained Belgian draft horses. Four horses harnessed and hitched to a wagon require serious driving skills and experience. Harrington was the last entrant in the parade, and he believed he and his teams were ready to put on a show.

The wagon was huge, new, and glittering with the gold letters of Harrington's farm name. He sat on the driver's seat, his fists full of reins, outfitted in his flashy western costume and ten-gallon hat. The abundant silver on the harnesses blazed and shimmered in the sun. Two big men stood at the heads of the lead team, putting all the strength and commands they could muster into keeping the four colossal Belgians from bolting. They reared, neighed, and threw their heads around in their effort to be free of the confining harness they plainly were not accustomed to.

The livestock part of the parade was just starting to slowly round the last half of the racetrack which lay along the swamp-edged river. Harrington could wait no longer to exhibit his expertise and daring with a four-horse hitch. He rose from his seat to heighten his dramatic moment and, raising the reins, brought them down heavily on the near team's rumps as he roared to the two men, "Cut 'em loose!"

The men barely managed to jump aside as the enormous horses leaped skyward, front hooves churning the air, then came down onto the track in a full-speed gallop. Harrington was thrown backward on the seat and lost most of his clutch on the reins as his tall hat went spiraling off into the distance. The teams were uncontrolled runaways. Harrington was bucking around, half on the seat, trying to hold on with one hand while reaching for a few more reins with the other.

The crowd was horrified as the great mass of horse flesh and wagon approached the plodding livestock on the other side of the track. Jim was shouting with his microphone to all people and children on the track ahead to get off anywhere they could. Most headed for the swamp alongside the river and, miraculously, there were no injuries of people or livestock, although all had been severely frightened. Harrington and his teams went around the racetrack many times before the horses were finally exhausted enough to be caught by the two farm hands.

The fair's livestock superintendent, who was livid with rage and fright at what could have happened, said to Harrington, "If brains were dynamite you couldn't blow your nose!" He went on to tell him what he thought of his ancestry and intelligence, further commanding him never to show his face on Union Fairgrounds again.

On the last night of the fair, the auto thrill drivers roared past our camper's bedroom window, gunning their unmuffled engines to further excite the crowd. After the show, the grounds settled into peaceful silence. It was interrupted only by the endearing hoots of an owl in a nearby tree and the night-haunting calls of the loons, perhaps the most lonely and beautiful sound in the north country. This special fair, surrounded by blueberry hills and lakes, was over until next year.

SAILING SIDEWAYS

Aside from rowing a dory in my childhood and experience with power boats in later years, I know nothing about sailing. I admire the beauty of it, especially the silence that is broken only by the wind and water rushing along the hull. There must be deep satisfaction and joy in meeting the challenge of harnessing wind as one's power source.

Learning to sail has to involve knowing your particular vessel as well as the general science of sailing. While our boat was berthed at a river marina some years ago, we witnessed an example of a sailboat owner laboring to understand his boat. She had been delivered by truck, so this was his first experience with her. The gentleman had bought a sailboat that was not born and bred in northern waters. Her beam was narrow for her length and her mast was too tall for her shallow draft. She was not designed for Maine seas. She appeared to be an old southern shellfishing boat. The vessel was a maverick and hard to handle. She luffed and shuddered, laid over too hard for prevailing conditions, and ended up flowing beam-to with the river's current daily, her sails slack and whipping regardless of the owner's efforts.

The captain and his friend planned a passage south with this boat and he spent several weeks trying to get his "sideways ship" under control. Apparently there was a time frame involved for this trip, because when the day came for departure it was an absolute ready-or-not endeavor.

Fuel for the auxiliary engine was first. There was a good wind as the captain headed for the fuel dock, but it wasn't working for this little vessel. He spent the better part of an hour tacking and struggling to sail the short distance to the fuel dock. White-faced and tight-lipped, he finally touched the dock and shouted to his friend to quickly cast a dock line. The gentleman friend obliged with a mighty fling and the dockhand grabbed the line.

All of the line. Including the bitter end. The friend had neglected to secure one end of the line to the boat, which was now rapidly floating away from the dock. The captain, stressed and frustrated by his long, awkward approach to the fuel dock, roared to his friend, "You stupid, backward idiot! Tie some lines to those cleats! Any ox-brained clod would have known that much!" The friend and the captain were retired from distinguished professions and were close to the same age.

The sailboat drifted away quickly and for a long distance. Another hour of tedious effort to approach the dock ensued. This time, the lines were properly attached. The captain's mood had become even worse. He snarled to his friend, "Grab the fuel key, you numb dullard!"

The friend scrambled midship and attempted to use the fuel key. He reported meekly, "It doesn't fit." Captain bawled, "It's the wrong one, you witless imbecile! Go below and fetch the right one! I'm going to kick the skillety shit out of you, sorry sod that you are!" This was followed by more loud and salty threats that hung in the air like smoke. Nobody around the docks could help hearing him, as he bellowed at mega levels.

Fueled and ready as she would ever be, the misbegotten little boat floundered sideways down the river on her way south. We all wondered how the captain's friend was going to survive the trip without jumping ship at the first opportunity. Months later, there was word from him. They did eventually reach their destination after many disasters. The first disaster was they had forgotten all about provisioning their ship with food and they went hungry until they could find a facility where they could dock the boat.

Ducks in the Desert

No matter how happy we are with where we live, traveling to other parts of our great nation is enlightening, as we can observe differences in people's ways of life as well as the great contrasts in the geography of this country. Maine and Arizona are a fine example. Both are very beautiful in their own unique way, which we have seen on a few trips out West.

On a journey to Arizona one winter, we met a person who will always remain in our memory. We were camped at Apache Junction, which is surrounded by the Superstition Mountains. Other than the mountains, the countryside consists mostly of desert with abundant growths of prickly pear cactus, ocatilla, mesquite, and other low-growing vegetation.

Missing the sight of water, we went to visit Canyon Lake, which nestles deep within towering, starkly bare rock cliffs. The lake is actually the result of the Salt River being dammed to form a narrow lake twelve miles long and ninety feet deep in some places. It seemed so strange to see a lake in such harsh surroundings without the soft green of the pines and hemlock that border our Maine lakes. Instead, there was just austere gray and brown walls of rock with bleak desert beyond.

While waiting for a boat ride on the lake, we walked around the docks where an amazing amount of pleasure boats were tied up. Ducks swam with a lone domestic goose. There were many dark birds with round bodies, white beaks, and fairly long legs. There were no webs on their feet, but when they entered the water they swam as well as the ducks.

Approaching one of the small marina's few docks, we saw a tall, slender man surrounded by both land and water birds. When he finished throwing food onto the dock for them, we asked him about what we called the "webless-footed birds" and how they swam so well. He smiled and said, "I'll show you!" Explaining that they were called marsh or mud hens or "coots" locally, he opened a loaf of bread from his cart, held out a slice, and called a name. A marsh hen ran up and took it gently from his hand. Now we could see its feet. There were no webs between the toes, but each toe and its legs were covered with very large scales that would obviously open in the water and be an efficient aid to swimming.

The kindly man introduced himself as David, the marina's custodian, a job he had held for many years. David's eyes were bright with delight as he told us about all of the land and water birds and how he fed them several times a day. It was plain that he provided the food himself. He had named many of the birds, and some sat on his shoulders.

David had a special relationship with a lone goose. He was a gander, and David had named him Ozzie. For twenty-five years Ozzie had a mate named Nellie. Both geese could be picked up by David. He said they would nestle against his chest and nibble gently at his face. This is rare behavior for domestic geese and a tribute to the rapport that David had built with the birds.

One day, Ozzie and Nellie didn't arrive for their morning food and weren't seen for several days. David took a rowboat and went searching. He found Nellie floating, lifelessly entangled in a fisherman's line. Ozzie was staying close to her in grief and dismay. David took them both home. Now, Ozzie hangs out with half a dozen of his favorite ducks and continues to enjoy being cuddled by David each day.

David told us he came to work one morning and thought Ozzie was a goner. A bobcat was standing on a shore rock holding Ozzie underwater, and the gander was about to drown. Before David could intervene, Ozzie blasted himself out of the water, knocking the bobcat off balance and into the water. Ozzie beat the bobcat on the face with his wings until the cat fled from the lake and off into the mountains.

The setting for this lake had its own kind of beauty in a forbidding kind of way—lonely distances, treeless and severe. The warmth and life the place provided for David year after year was his interaction with his birds. We will always remember his gentle face and voice and the special smile in his eyes when he spoke of his cherished friends.

THE PIED PIPER OF PIGS

Our good friends Fred and Brenda owned a nice property for raising animals, and they decided that buying a few pigs would be a good start. They bought half-grown stock, six sows (females), and one boar (male). The pigs had a comfortable building and a large yard.

One brisk December day, the pigs found an appropriately sized escape route in their yard fence and were compelled to explore the big world that lay beyond their enclosure. The paved road was nearby, and it beckoned as the ideal place to begin a journey. Some time later a neighbor telephoned Fred, who was working at home, to tell him the pigs were headed down the road in a southerly direction.

Brenda was at work, so Fred knew he would be the Lone Ranger in this looming debacle. He jumped into their spare car and drove south. A mile or so later, he spied the pigs. They were not straggling along, but were lined up six abreast and marching with purpose as if in a military formation. Fortunately, traffic was scarce, but trying to catch six young pigs by oneself is a daunting task.

Fred figured the boar was the most friendly and that if he caught it, the rest would follow him. Fred is a big strong fellow, so he managed to get hold of the boar. He tucked the squirming pig firmly under one arm and opened the car's trunk, planning to put him in it, shut it, and catch the sows hovering nearby.

But Christmas was a few days away. Brenda had decided the trunk of this car they seldom used was a fine place to hide all her

Christmas shopping, including gifts for Fred. The trunk was stuffed full of wrapped presents.

Standing with a screaming, struggling pig under one arm, Fred couldn't imagine how he was going to empty the trunk contents into the back seat package by package. However he accomplished the task just that way, because he knew it wouldn't be easy to catch the boar a second time. When all the gifts were in the rear seat, Fred shoved the boar into the trunk and slammed the lid.

Looking at the attitude of the sows, he didn't believe he could successfully catch them without continuous escapes. However, Fred noted the sows' concern for the boar, their leader, as they listened to him squealing and screeching in his confinement. He then gambled that they would follow the car. Fred slowly drove toward home with five sows obediently following close behind the car. A vehicle that had come behind Fred along the way stopped as Fred made his turn into his driveway. The man in the vehicle laughingly shouted that he had never seen a sight this comical and couldn't wait to get home to tell all about it. Because of the loyalty of pigs to their barn mates, this potential fiasco ended well.

HAUL-OUT TIME

Our boating years are over, but longing and memories remain. It always seemed that summer flashed past our outreaching arms. We were suddenly in the season of the blue enamel skies of October, creamy granite shorelines caressed by now crimson huckleberry and blueberry bushes and the quiet dark of juniper. The inexorable passage of months had brought us to haul-out time for our boat *Come Spring*. She bore that name because we would talk all winter about launching again come spring. Now she had to leave the sea and be brought out to spend the winter on the "hard."

No more looking at islands rising through the fog in blurred majesty or sleeping in the lift, drop, and roll of the incoming tide while nestled in a snug berth. No waking up at breaking dawn surrounded by a harbor's satin sheet of rose shot with silver and edged by dark spruce-shadow. We must wait to bring the coffee out to the cockpit, inhale balsam, bayberry, salt, and sea roses, watch the ospreys and plan the day's destination.

Memories flood the mind with pictures of island shores, when we felt like we were the first ones ever to find these wild and uninhabited places. They are inspired by the calls of gulls, diving guillemots, and mats of beach pea vines that hide the nesting sandpipers until they rush out peeping shrilly to lead the intruder away, comically elevating their tiny rumps as they run. We remember finding treasures of sea-carved driftwood, mussel shells turned delicate lavender by the sun, a moment of dreaming about what it would be like to just live here, to stay here forever in this serene beauty.

Then back to the home harbor, all boats dipping their bows in reverence to the changing tides that they always face in unison. Power and sailboats. Mostly lobster boats that, to me, are the most noble of vessels ever built. They differ in lines, bow height, and beam, but always with that sweet sweep of shear and sea-challenging structure that gets them out there to work and survive through all seasons in Maine's quickly changing waters.

In summer harbors the slap of halyards on the sailboat masts is gentle, monotonously musical—in fall, rapid and mournful. The shrouds sometimes softly shriek a disconsolate melody in an easterly wind, a song of the ferocity of winter storms to come. The masts will be laid to rest on racks by then, and again in spring they will resume their riggings' siren call to the sea. Then the boats will rear and tug at their moorings like horses at the end of their lunge tethers. The golden summer skies will be so clear the Milky Way is reflected in sea darkness. Stars hang from the heavens like unshed tears.

Haul-out time is hard on the spirit. It is the beginning of counting the months until spring launching, when our yearnings will be quenched by the activities of readying the boat, painting, scraping, polishing teak, attending to engines. As someone once said of this phase: "What is better than messing about with boats?"

REVERIE

The white-hot sun of August is now gold, skies are deeper blue, and shadows slide over the lawn sooner in the day. Goldenrod, purple asters, and Queen Anne's lace skirt the road verges.

Pearl gray mists of early morning hover over the fields, turning to honey and smoke in the rising sun, just as they did when we showed sheep at Farmington Fair. Soon after dawn, teamsters were driving their pulling horses through the surrounding pastures, exercising for the night's contests. Puffs of steam drifted from the horses' velvet noses as they leaned into the load. Teamsters stood on their stone drags, hands full of reins, their connection to horse-might.

Brooks and streams are now in slow leisure waiting for the fall rains to help them rush their waters to the sea. Hummingbirds and bees dart anxiously over fading flowers, searching for new blossoms that have not yet yielded their tiny offerings of nectar.

The rapid *click-tick* sound of crickets signals the changing season. They burrow in the grass to evade crows or find a hidden corner in the house to share their peaceful song of late summer. Small red blushes of maple branches peer timidly through the green hardwoods, promising a full-blown entrance soon.

Earth's riches of fruit, gardens, and second-crop hay are briskly harvested. Pitch-coated pine cones hang high and heavily from tall pines. Legend says abundant evergreen cones forecast a hard winter. We are Maine. We will be ready.

Salt & Roses Acknowledgements

I am grateful to Islandport Press Publisher, Dean Lunt, Piper Wilber, and Shannon Butler for their editing expertise, their great support, unfailing cooperation, kindness, and help. Thank you! I also thank Suzi Thayer for her lovely painting that graces the cover of *Salt and Roses*.

Warm thanks to the wonderful Roberts family, publishers of *The Lincoln County News* for the last one-hundred years. This newspaper began its support of our communities in 1875. It has been my privilege to have had my column "Lower Round Pond" appear in this fine publication for the last sixty-plus years!